SA
SEX

SANE
SEX

Christian
thinking on
sexuality

General Editor Francis Foulkes

ANZEA

SANE SEX
Copyright © 1993 Francis Foulkes

Anzea books are published by
ANZEA PUBLISHERS
3–5 Richmond Road
Homebush West NSW 2140
Australia

Cover design by Buzz Creative, Brisbane
Typeset by DOCUPRO, Sydney
Printed in Australia by Griffin Paperbacks, Netley, S.A.

ISBN 0-85892-526-5

◆ Contents ◆

The writers

All of the writers of this book are New Zealanders. While they have a special concern for their own context, they have tried to keep in mind a wider range of contexts.

Colin Becroft, an Agnlican layman, practises as a psychotherapist in Auckland. He is a clinical member of the American Association for Marriage and Family Therapy. He has served as a staff member of Scripture Union in New Zealand, Australia and the United States.

Neil Broom is New Zealand Health Research Council Senior Research Fellow in Biomechanics at Auckland University. He has a special interest in the interplay between science and human behaviour.

Marjorie and Francis Foulkes have trained men and women for ministry and for cross-cultural mission in Nigeria, Australia and New Zealand. Until recently Francis, an ordained Anglican minister, was Warden of St.John's Theological College, Auckland. He is the author of a number of Bible commentaries.

Grant Gillett is Associate Professor of Medical Ethics in the University of Otago Medical School and a practising neurosurgeon. His writings, in the fields of medical ethics, philosophy and psychology, include *Reasonable care* (Bristol Press, 1989) and *Representation, meaning and thought* (Oxford University Press, 1992).

Ian Hooker is an ordained minister of the Congregational Union of New Zealand, with considerable pastoral experience assisting people struggling with homosexuality. He helped establish Exodus Ministries in Auckland and was its chairperson.

Peter Lineham has never married. He is a senior lecturer in History at Massey University and has a doctorate from the University of Sussex. He is the author of a number of books and has been deeply involved in the work of Scripture Union, the Tertiary Students' Christian Fellowship and the Christian Brethren Research Fellowship.

Ivan Moses has worked as a secondary and tertiary teacher. His last appointment was as Director of the Auckland Institute of Technology. A Presbyterian layman, he has been President of the Bible College of New Zealand, Scripture Union and the Tertiary Students' Christian Fellowship (N.Z.).

Sheila Pritchard has never married. She

was a primary school teacher in New Zealand, and then a missionary in Nigeria. She is currently in charge of Spiritual Formation programs in the Bible College of New Zealand.

Dr John and Mrs Agnes Sturt have been marriage counsellors and leaders of marriage enrichment retreats for 15 years. In 1978 they established the Christian Care Centre in Auckland, an inter-denominational medical and counselling agency committed to total health care. For 20 years they were medical missionaries in Papua New Guinea.

Harold Turner is a Presbyterian minister who worked in Dunedin as a tertiary chaplain and in halls of residence, then taught theology and religious studies in universities in Africa, America and Britain. He returned to New Zealand in 1989 and established the Gospel and Cultures Trust for 'deep mission' to our culture.

The editor expresses appreciation for the help in editing this volume given by Colin Becroft and also Frank Walton, a secondary teacher in South Auckland.

◆ CHAPTER 1 ◆

The quest for guidelines

FRANCIS FOULKES

The time in which we live has been called a 'sex-mad age'. Certainly it is an age in which the mass media—TV programs, videos, advertising, popular magazines—and much fiction frequently picture sex as the commodity that is to be desired above almost everything else; and sex is alleged to bring the greatest satisfaction to life. Yet at the same time relationships between the sexes are the cause of many people's greatest sorrows and distress. Some may say cynically, Has it not been like that from the dawn of time—joy and sorrow, love and hate, harmony and conflict? It is also an age of sexual revolution, in which modern methods of contraception have played a major part. So has the challenge to traditionally accepted roles for women and men. The world-wide AIDS epidemic now adds a sinister dimension. Never has western society experienced so acutely the battle of the sexes, sexual abuse, the dehumanising of women by pornography, the violence of men against women and children. In addition, there is all the pain of broken relationships, unwanted children, children with only one parent to care for them.

What can we do, what should we do? Is there any formula for experiencing the blessings of our sexuality while avoiding the anguish?

Christian people look to the pages of the Bible for the foundation principles of their faith and life-style. Most Christians agree at least in seeing in both Old and New Testaments the two supreme principles of love (for God and for other people) and justice. There are differences, it is true, between the presentation of the Law in the Old Testament and the way of Christ in the New. The New Testament lacks the expression of penalties, and the detailed laws, that we have in the Old. It is also true that many things in the Bible were written to meet particular situations. In using the Bible, therefore, we must try to see what applied to a particular social and cultural situation and is only applicable in principle beyond it, and what guidelines remain true and should be applied today, whatever our race or culture.

There is a tendency today, in matters relating to right and wrong in human conduct, to begin where society is, and to try to see the best way through the problems that we are facing. Yet if, as we believe, there are God-given guidelines, we are surely wise to begin with them. We should hesitate to write off too readily what the Bible says as belonging to another age and another culture. The wisdom of the Bible has stood the test of many generations and brought transforming application to many different cultural situations. It is in this spirit that these studies in human sexuality turn to the Bible, and seek to understand the purposes of God shown there and above all in Jesus Christ.

It is not our aim to win arguments by offering proof texts, nor to be judgmental of others. We all fail in many ways to live up to the high standards set for Christian people. Our desire is to show that there is a divine purpose for marriage and family relationships, and that God's counsel relating to the expression of our sexuality, whether we are single or married, is intended for our highest well-being. In his wisdom and love, God our Maker has provided instruction as to how we, his creatures should use our minds and bodies. We have God's assurance of the support of the Holy Spirit to enable us all, whether men or women, to follow the way of life to which we are called and to help us to attain our fullest potential as individuals and in society.

Are these guidelines only for those who profess the Christian faith? Although the argument cannot be developed here, our conviction is that the basic principles set out in Scripture are intended for the well-being of all humankind, for each of us individually, for our family groups, and for society as a whole.

We begin by presenting an overview of the Bible's teaching about our sexuality, and continue with the consideration of home and family, marriage and singleness. Sexually transmitted diseases and the question of 'safe sex' are dealt with by writers who have expertise on these subjects. The subject of homosexuality is discussed by two people with pastoral and professional counselling experience. A chapter is given to the consideration of some deeper ethical and theological considerations, especially in relation to homosexuality. There is a measure of overlap in the different contributions to the book, but we trust a coherency in the whole.

◆ CHAPTER 2 ◆

Sexuality and the purposes of God

MARJORIE AND FRANCIS FOULKES

The love of man for woman and woman for man has been celebrated throughout the ages and across the world's varied cultures. Loveliness and beauty, devotion and sacrifice, are evoked in the lyrical and passionate celebration of our human sexuality. What ideal of human love is more beautiful than that of a man and a woman committed to and delighting in each other! And one of the loveliest examples of that love in all the world is that of a couple whose faithful partnership has remained unbroken over many years, having endured all the ups and downs, the joys and sorrows that life brings.

Yet the Christian church has often given confused messages about human partnership, and in different ways it does so still. Sometimes religious people have attached shame and guilt to sexual relationships as such. Marriage has, in the past, been seen as a second best to celibacy, or sexual intercourse as necessary merely for the propagation of the human race, and not as an expression of love and joy and delight. Today, while some fence sexual relationships around with strict rules, many more reckon any sexual expression involving consent as good and acceptable.

People probably experience more sexual freedom now than ever before. Yet this increase of freedom has brought more broken relationships, violence and unhappiness than ever. Every wedding is a promise of great joy, and there are some wonderfully happy homes, but in most western societies they are in a minority. While it takes two to bring a child into being, statistics show that a large percentage of all family units in our society are headed by solo parents. What has gone wrong? Some blame unemployment. But even with all the unemployment of the

Great Depression of the 1930s, it was not like this.

We write out of the conviction that we have been given divine guidelines for life and love. They are found in the Bible, expressed in a way that we can understand and intended by a loving and caring God for our greatest good. We neglect them to our own great loss. For true freedom is not freedom to do what we each want, but freedom to choose the highest and best. The teaching of the Bible is, we believe, relevant to the understanding of our sexuality and never more so than in this last decade of the 20th century. In the Bible we may not find detailed answers to all the difficult and complex questions that may be asked today; but there we do find important guidelines to direct us. Arrangements for marriage and family life may differ greatly in our different cultures, yet the teaching of Scripture provides basic principles applicable to us all.

THE BIBLE'S FIRST CHAPTER

In the first chapter of Genesis we read of God creating everything in the universe, and giving to humanity a unique place in all creation. People are described as being made 'in the image of God'. This means no less than being made for a special relationship

with God, able to hear God's word, to understand God's purpose, to speak to God in
prayer. Male and female alike are made in
the image of God. So our sexuality—our
existence as male and female—should be celebrated as a good gift of God. Human life is
sustained and made rich and beautiful by the
relationship between man and woman. In
Genesis 1 man and woman are told, 'be fruitful and multiply': children are conceived and
born out of that relationship. Shared joy,
shared responsibility—and as well a shared
accountability for the rest of creation—are all
implied in Genesis 1.

THE SECOND CHAPTER

Genesis 1 emphasises the creation of
humanity in the image of God and speaks of
people (like other living creatures) being
fruitful and multiplying. Genesis 2 emphasises the partnership and companionship of
man and woman without specially mention-
ing the conception and birth of children. The
statement that it is not good for one person
to be alone indicates that all human companionship is honoured and intended to enrich
our lives. This is especially true of the companionship between man and woman, who
are equal, but different, and intended to
help, complement and support each other.

Genesis 2 goes on to speak of man and woman becoming 'one flesh' together. This relationship is described in terms of a man (singular) leaving his father and mother and clinging to his wife (singular), and the *two* becoming *one* flesh (Genesis 2:24). A later chapter in this book will enlarge on what that means for marriage. It is sufficient to say here that Scripture celebrates the beauty of that one flesh relationship and the great joy it brings to both partners. There are examples in the Bible of that partnership of love and joy, and innumerable couples in very diverse societies all over the world have confirmed the truth of the biblical model, finding joy and satisfaction as they have given themselves to each other in loving and lasting partnership.

In this chapter we take further the far-reaching implications of the words of Genesis 2:24 about 'one flesh' relationships. These words are basic for the teaching of the Law and the Prophets in the Old Testament. They are also repeated and endorsed by Jesus himself in the New Testament. When people came to him with questions about divorce, Jesus made these words his reference point. He said, 'From the beginning of creation, "God made them male and female". "For this reason a man shall leave his father and mother and be joined to his wife, and the two shall become one flesh." So they are no longer two but one flesh' (Mark 10:7-8—see also Matthew 19:4-6). These words are repeated later in the New Testament, in Ephesians 5:31, where teaching is given about relationships in marriage.

WHAT ABOUT POLYGAMY?

Some may say, 'How is it that we read so much in the Old Testament about polygamy?' Many societies all through history have adopted this practice. The Old Testament often describes polygamous relationships, from Abraham onwards, just as it also describes situations where one marriage partner is unfaithful to the other. We also read of terrible instances of the violence of men against women. All such things come in the Bible's *descriptions* of the realities of life, life that misses God's best and is often very sordid. The Bible's *prescription* is different. That prescription is the one-to-one partnership of equals. Polygamy falls short of God's purpose, and the Old Testament clearly shows the difficulties that it creates, including rivalries between co-wives and their children who have to compete for a husband's or a father's affection and support.

Those who take the gospel to polygamous

societies need great wisdom. In the past they have sometimes acted unwisely in the way that they have dealt with the polygamous social order that they have found. Nevertheless countless Christian people from such backgrounds have come to appreciate the vast change that takes place when a wife comes to be seen as a partner, not as a possession and not one of several wives. In particular, women from those backgrounds have acknowledged the liberating transformation that the gospel of Christ and the teaching of the Bible have brought them.

Those of us who live in societies where polygamy is not the custom should be slow to criticise. An African bishop friend once put it to us, 'People in our society certainly practised polygamy, but in western society you have serial polygamy'.

Our mass media, television, videos and the cinema constantly put before us a picture of sexual relationships that is very different from the biblical ideal. They show sexual relationships as often casually entered into, and set aside with equal casualness, while very rarely giving any indication of the suffering caused. Advertising blatantly exploits sexuality and depersonalises both women and men. Pornography has become a thriving industry.

PARTNERSHIP

Genesis 2 presents the ideal of true partnership between the sexes, and the joy intended in the one-to-one relationship of marriage, where there is commitment and trust. By contrast, where one seeks satisfaction at the expense of the other, there is an uncaring exploitation of the other person and a misuse of the good and lovely gifts that God has given. The one-to-one partnership in marriage involves the sharing of life by equals—two who are equally made in God's image, equal in status, and each complementary to the other.

Genesis 3 shows that it is the result of human sinfulness and male pride that a man 'rules over' a woman. Today we see the extreme expression of this rule in man's violence towards woman, violence that is physical, psychological and emotional. This has debased women, treating them as sexual objects rather than as persons. It stands therefore as part and parcel of human fallenness and sin.

That human fallenness affects us all in all of our relationships. While men spoil the partnership that God intended by their desire to dominate, we can say (without stereotyping gender roles) that women also have their characteristic ways of spoiling the partnership. None of us are free from blame. But the partnership that has been spoiled by our selfishness can be restored by God's forgiveness and help. The ideal of renewed partnership, and the principle of male-female equality are expressed by the apostle Paul in Galatians 3:28, 'There is no longer Jew or Greek, there is no longer slave or free, there is no longer male and female; for all of you are one in Christ Jesus.' Whatever is said of the different roles of husband and wife, the prior principle of the equality of man and woman as persons stands. A passage that has often been misunderstood in what it says about husbands and wives—Ephesians 5:22-33—begins by calling each to submit to the other, and challenges the husband to love his wife with a sacrificial love comparable with the way 'Christ loved the church and gave himself up for her'. In 1 Corinthians 7:3-5 Paul speaks of the complete mutuality of sexual relationships in marriage, on the basis of the husband and wife realising that each belongs to the other.

PROMISCUITY

The ready availability of condoms in western society makes an assumption that few people question. The assumption is one of freedom for sexual expression without any need for sexual partners to be committed to each other. A recent news item mentioned the tens of thousands of condoms that were available for the athletes who would spend just a few days at the Olympic Games. There is agitation for condoms to be readily available for teenagers in our secondary schools. The media and the heroes of contemporary music tell young people that it is good to experiment with sex before or instead of being tied to a lasting relationship in marriage. Adults often present a double standard, saying one thing but living out another.

Anyone who takes the Bible seriously, however, must be prepared to reckon with a different way of thinking, which is not merely a 'Thou shalt not'. The Bible has a deep respect for people as persons, not just sexual partners. We have referred to the words of the apostle Paul in 1 Corinthians 7. In the previous chapter of that letter he speaks against trivialising sexual relationships. Promiscuity and prostitution are not only a misuse of the human body, they are essentially depersonalising. Sexual relationships are intended to express the deep commitment and love between a man and woman.

The primary application of the passage is

to those who acknowledge themselves to be Christians and so can be asked, 'Do you not know that your bodies are members of Christ?—Or do you not know that your body is a temple of the Holy Spirit?' (1 Corinthians 6:15,19). The principle, however, is applicable to all people, not only to those who are Christians. To be joined with another in sexual relationship is to become 'one body' with that person. Two lives are brought together in the most intimate way. Sexual intercourse is intended to be the physical expression of mutual commitment of life.[1] This is God's purpose in respect of human partnership. It is also God's purpose that the conception of children should arise from the deep love of one person for another. Such children are born to two parents who are committed to each other and to them.

While sexual relationship is intended to bring joy and blessing to the partners, it is not to be reduced to casual play. Sex is irresponsible when there is no regard for its emotional and psychological effect on the life of either partner. Nor should it ever ignore the potential for a new human life to be conceived (since no contraceptive method is perfectly reliable).

PERMANENT PARTNERSHIP

It is well known that the percentage of

marriages ending in divorce has steadily increased, especially in western countries. In many countries law reform has made it easier to obtain divorce, and thus couples facing difficulties have often been less inclined to work at them and more ready to break up. Also many couples now prefer de facto relationships, or, if they marry, reckon from the beginning on a way out if the marriage should run into difficulties.

The service of Christian marriage reflects the teaching of the Bible when it calls both partners to be faithful to the other 'as long as you both shall live'. The Seventh Commandment, against adultery (Exodus 20:14 and Deuteronomy 5:18), is rightly considered central to Old Testament morality, and it is endorsed in the New Testament. The prophets spoke against adultery and the breakdown of marriage. The Book of Proverbs (e.g. 6:20-35) contains strong words about marital faithfulness. It is true that the Old Testament law made provision for divorce (Deuteronomy 24), and clearly the laws of any country must do likewise. Yet divorce is always a failure to realise the highest purpose of God. As Jesus put it, the law about divorce was added 'because of your hardness of heart'. 'What God has joined together' he said, 'let no one separate' (Mark 10: 5,9).

The Christian church has to deal compassionately and sensitively with those whose marriages have broken down. We acknowledge the forgiving grace of God and uphold the possibility of new beginnings. Yet we cannot but regard with great seriousness the vast increase in marriage breakdowns in our society. We must recognise with deepest concern the suffering that this causes to the separating partners, still more to the children of the broken marriage (and indeed the following generation).

SINGLENESS

While the Bible's teaching on sexuality and on marriage belong closely together, single people are not regarded as missing out on the good purposes of God. To remain single does not mean necessarily that a person will fail to find fulfilment in life. The teaching of Jesus indicates that some may make the costly choice to live a single life for the sake of the kingdom of God (Matthew 19:12). Christian history is full of examples of those who have done this, and have found a life that is both personally fulfilling and of immense blessing to others. Above all, we have the model of the life of Jesus himself.

Singleness is dealt with from two different standpoints in chapters 5 and 6.

HOMOSEXUALITY

Some in our society today call for homosexual and heterosexual relationships to be seen as equally 'natural' and 'acceptable'. Others (not necessarily people who are specially influenced by Christian teaching) are aghast at the thought. The writers of this book are concerned that all we say is said in love and with the respect that we owe to those in homosexual relationships as to all others in the human family. Homophobia is not a Christian attitude. It is, however, the concern of many Christian people today that biblical statements are often too readily being put on one side as not relevant to our modern situation and our culture.

In the Old Testament law, Leviticus 18:22 and 20:13 are the particular passages that deal with homosexual practices. It is sometimes argued that the context is the refutation of idolatrous pagan practices (especially those that went on in heathen sanctuaries, such as male prostitution). Some argue that when homosexual acts are spoken of as 'an abomination', this is only a ritual or cultic regulation that is not relevant to consenting homosexual relationships today. It is true that the people of Israel were called to a life-style different from that of the nations around them. We should notice, however, that Leviticus chapters 18-20 includes both religious and ethical laws. In addition to the laws about sexual relationships, there are those that forbid stealing, giving unjust judgments, and taking revenge on an enemy. The forbidden sexual relationships include incest, adultery, homosexual acts and sexual relationships with animals. It is much fairer to the context to say that the basic principle implied is that expressed in Genesis 2:24; the prohibitions follow from it.

There is no direct reference to homosexual practices in the Gospels. In the remainder of the New Testament three passages in the Epistles refer to homosexuality: Romans 1:24-27, 1 Corinthians 6:9 and 1 Timothy 1:10. The rare Greek word (*arsenokoites* = going to bed with a male) used in 1 Corinthians and 1 Timothy reflects the Greek (Septuagint) translation of the Leviticus passages. The Romans passage regards homosexual practices, along with many other sins, as one way among others in which humanity has distorted God's created order and rejected the Creator's plan. Thus Paul speaks of homosexual acts as an offence against our creation, an 'exchanging of natural intercourse for unnatural'. Some have argued that here the apostle is merely drawing on a list of vices such as ancient moralists regularly used in their teaching. In principle and in detailed application, however, Paul's ethical teaching has a greater seriousness than that. Nor is it convincing to argue that the apostle was referring simply to male prostitution or to paederasty (adults abusing young boys). He speaks first of the way that 'women exchanged natural intercourse for unnatural'. There can be little doubt that homosexual acts in general are referred to in this passage. It is also important to add that 1 Corinthians 6:9 implies that there were those previously involved in homosexual practices (and other conduct contrary to the rule of God) who were so involved no longer.

Consideration of both the biblical passages and the way we are made surely justifies the conclusion reached by the House of Bishops of the Church of England in a recent statement:

> Homophile orientation and its expression in sexual activity do not constitute a parallel and alternative form of human sexuality as complete within the terms of the created order as the heterosexual. The

convergence of Scripture, tradition and reasoned reflection on experience, even including the newly sympathetic and perceptive thinking of our own day, makes it impossible for the Church to come with integrity to any other conclusion. Heterosexuality and homosexuality are not equally congruous with the observed order of creation or with the insights of revelation as the Church engages with these in the light of her pastoral ministry.'[2]

JUDGMENTALISM OR LOVE

Those who set forward the biblical ideals for marriage and sexual relationships are often accused of being judgmental towards those who have not lived by those ideals. They are, in fact, easily made the butt of the judgmentalism of their critics. Judgmentalism all too readily functions both ways, and there is only one way out of it—the way of love. Love truly seeks the understanding and the fulfillment—for ourselves first of all, and then for others—of God's wise and loving purposes for humanity. Jesus accepted all who came to him and sought out those whom others (not least religious people) rejected. But where people were involved in following a way contrary to God's way, whether in dishonesty, hypocrisy or sexual relationships, he said to them, in effect, 'Go and sin no more'. He accepts and is always ready to forgive us when we have fallen short of God's standards; that means all of us. But then he calls us to make changes in our lives, changes based on the guidelines of love given to us in the Scriptures.

NOTES

1. Psychiatrist Jack Dominian, in his book *Sexual integrity* (Darton, Longman and Todd, 1988), chapters 5-7, gives cogent reasons, based on an understanding of psychology and human development, against promiscuous sexual intercourse where there is no life commitment of those involved.

2. *Issues of human sexuality*, A statement by the House of Bishops of the General Synod of the Church of England, December 1991 (Church House Publishing), p.40.

◆ CHAPTER 3 ◆

The home and family

IVAN MOSES

This chapter has two aims. First, to show what is good and beautiful in the Christian ideal of the family (as set forth in the Bible), and what it offers to individuals, couples, children and society. Second, to indicate what happens when the teachings of Scripture are no longer followed.

Few joys in life can be compared with that of parents when a strong, healthy baby is born. The mother, as the Gospel writer puts it, is able to forget the pain of childbirth because of the joy of having brought a child into the world (John 16:21). The father shares in the joy, marvelling that he has helped to produce the new bundle of life, which brings so much love with it. Family and friends rejoice too, perhaps recognising the child as a gift of God. The happiness of home life is intended by God for all to know and experience. Happiness, however, is a by-product of something deeper, especially if it is to persist through the strains of living.

WHAT IS 'FAMILY'?

Before we look at the things that produce happiness in the home, we should define what is meant by 'family'. Different cultures offer different answers. We can speak first of the 'nuclear' family consisting of father, mother and children. Reference is made in other places in this book to the way that Genesis 2 speaks of a man leaving his father and mother to be joined to his wife. That is the basis of the family. The couple recognise that, from the time of that mutual commitment, their closest relationship and deepest loyalty are to each other.

We also speak of the 'extended family', which includes brothers, sisters, uncles and aunts, nieces and nephews and cousins, and especially grandparents. In some societies the functions and duties of these relatives are more clearly defined and valued than in some western countries. The inclusion of the different generations in the extended family means that old age is not something to be feared for the loneliness it brings. Instead, it is looked on as a stage of life where the wisdom learned by experience can be sought and shared. Grandparents also find great joy in their grandchildren. The Book of Ruth in the Old Testament beautifully illustrates this. The old grandmother, Naomi, had known much sorrow, but when a son was born to Ruth, her daughter-in-law, the elderly women said to Naomi, 'He shall be to you a restorer of life and a nourisher of your old age' (Ruth 4:15).

The Bible makes it clear that the family is part of God's loving purpose for humanity. It is protected by positive and negative teaching, both in Old and New Testaments. There is the negative commandment that stands guard over the marriage relationship and the family: 'You shall not commit adultery' (Exodus 20:14). The fifth of the Ten Commandments is positive: 'Honour your father and your mother'. With it, moreover, is linked the promise indicating that the nation whose family life is strong will itself endure (Exodus 20:12). The Old Testament commandments are not only reiterated in the New (Matthew 19:18 and Ephesians 6:1-3), but we have the beautiful example of the Holy Family in which our incarnate Lord grew up. The only record we have of Jesus' childhood tells of a journey to the temple in Jerusalem, after which he returned to Nazareth with Mary, his mother, and Joseph 'and was obedient to them . . . And Jesus increased in wisdom and in years, and in divine and human favour' (Luke 2:51-52).

BLESSINGS EXPERIENCED THROUGH THE CHRISTIAN FAMILY

The benefits and blessings of Christian family life have often been described and shown by example. They are well expressed in the statement of the House of Bishops of the Church of England that has been referred to already in this book. As our human sexuality is such a 'wonderful gift from God',

a man and a woman can be united in a relationship which for depth, intensity and joy is unique in their experience. They can find a strength and support in one another which helps each of them to mature as individuals. They can form a partnership which is both a blessing to the whole community and [a] stable and loving environment in which children need to be brought up. Being much more than simply physical organisms, they share their lives with one another at many different levels—bodily, emotional, intellectual, social and spiritual.[1]

Such a marriage partnership means that one supports the other in hard times such as sickness and unemployment. Children benefit unspeakably from growing up in such an environment. Society benefits too because this kind of relationship is not selfish, but can reach out to those in need.

This is clearly a very different model from others prevalent in our society today. Casual relationships offer sex but not necessarily love, while in many de facto relationships one party is not permanently committed to the other. Similarly 'trial' marriages, by the very definition, differ from permanent commitments. Such relationships are often regarded as arrangements to be entered into by mutual agreement, and severed in the same way. On the other hand the distinctive quality of Christian marriage, rightly understood, is that the partners enter into it responsibly as a loving contract with each other and with God. It involves the promise of a life-long relationship, and it is based on self-giving, not selfishness.

Yet God's blessings on marriage are not unconditional. The scriptures teach that God's will is for chastity before marriage, and exclusive faithfulness afterwards, as the promises made on the wedding day are worked through and kept. All this requires hard work, self-denial, a willingness to forgive and to be forgiven, and dependence on the grace and help of God. Partners must have a deep acceptance of one another as they work through their difficulties and as they pray for God's guidance and support. In marriage two people stand together loyally, uniting their gifts in service to their family and to others, sharing with each other at all levels.

THE TRAINING OF CHILDREN

Children are a gift from God to parents, but their coming lays on father and mother the privilege and the responsibility of training them to live good and useful lives. The Bible speaks of this in a number of different ways. The apostle Paul speaks of parents not provoking their children but rather encouraging them, leading them on with loving discipline and instruction.[2] Thus they can grow up healthy in mind and body, able to create a home of their own and to enrich society as they in their turn influence others for good. Such training calls for endless patience, and willingness to give time, thought and care.

Above all, the Bible emphasises that children should be brought up in the knowledge and love of God. In the Old Testament, Hebrew parents were constantly reminded that they should pass on to their children the story of what God had done for them, so that a vital faith in God would pass from generation to generation.[3] The greatest commandment of all was, 'You shall love the Lord your God with all your heart, and with all your soul, and with all your might', and the people were told, 'keep these words . . . Recite them to your children and talk about them when you are at home and when you are away, when you lie down and when you rise' (Deuteronomy 6:5-7). In this way what the psalmist speaks of is made possible: 'One generation shall laud your works to another, and shall declare your mighty acts' (Psalm 145:4). Christian parents have a similar responsibility, and the home is strong where the family reads the Scriptures and prays together in an atmosphere of loving acceptance. It has been well said that the family that prays together stays together.

The home is also the proper and ideal place for sex education. In ways appropriate to each stage of children's growth and development, they should be taught the meaning of their sexuality. No couples are perfect in their relationships, but they should aim to model partnership in love and respect and sensitivity. In the home healthy attitudes to same-sex friendships and opposite-sex friendships will be developed. Children will learn that the right context for intimate sexual relationship is where two people have a life commitment to each other. The father's attitude to his daughter will be such as to affirm her femininity, and he will model for his son how to relate to the opposite sex. The mother similarly will affirm and model attitudes for her son and daughter. Good example and good training in one generation will undoubtedly bear fruit in the next.

OUR CONTEMPORARY SITUATION

What have we done with the Bible's guidelines? In many western countries that have been deeply influenced in the past by loyalty to Christ and respect for the Scriptures, God's word is forgotten or ignored. People have largely turned their backs upon the church—and the church must carry substantial responsibility for that. We have to recognise our failure to be salt and light to the world (Matthew 5:13-14), and confess how we have neglected to be our 'brother's [and sister's] keeper'. Wherever the responsibility rests, inasmuch as the recipe God has given for the home has been neglected, we have witnessed disintegration in family life and in society—for the home provides the cement that holds society together.

Some years ago I was invited to a function where the home was being discussed. A Roman Catholic priest said, 'You cannot ignore the laws of God and expect to be happy any more than you can ignore the laws of health and expect to remain fit'. These words have stuck in my mind. The Old Testament prophets warned that a nation or people or society cannot continue to flourish if it disregards God's name and God's teaching. The history of Judah and Israel illustrates the fact that, when the prophets' warning was ignored, suffering inevitably followed. In the New Testament too there are clear warnings that, when people turn their backs on the God of righteousness, a catalogue of consequences follow. These consequences affect the mind and the body, the individual and the nation.

It is not my desire to write simplistically

about situations that are often complex. There are long-standing difficulties and problems that have deep roots in the past of our society. Where principles of justice and love have been neglected for generations, or are infringed today, there are inevitable consequences that impinge deeply on family life.

Ample statistical information available from a number of countries clearly indicates causes of the breakdown of family life and of violence within the family. They relate to those who have grown up from childhood never knowing the security offered by a home. Research recently carried out by the Australian Institute of Family Studies indicates a steady drift away from marriage during the past 25 years.[4] The Australian Summary of Statistics indicates that while the number of live births registered has been fairly constant, large numbers of children are born and grow up without the security of parents committed to each other and to the support of their children.[5]

A similar picture emerges in New Zealand. Recent research shows that barely 60 per cent of adults over 18 are married; that 1 in 6 persons are separated, divorced or living with a partner in a de facto relationship. There has been a rapid rise in numbers of teenage pregnancies and single-parent families, and more than one-third of babies born in 1990 were children of unmarried parents.[6] A Commission headed by a New Zealand High Court judge drew a frightening picture of many families: 'Contrary to the home being the place where support, protection and love are ensured, it has become the place where most violence occurs in society.'[7]

THE RESULT OF BREAKDOWN IN FAMILY LIFE

It must be allowed that some de facto relationships evidence a greater degree of commitment between partners than is evident in many marriages. I also gladly acknowledge that numbers of single or divorced parents show a high measure of responsibility to children. Yet the evidence from many different countries indicates that unstable, unhappy or broken homes are common in the lives of children in trouble or at risk. The report of the English House of Bishops, already quoted, observes,

Teachers and social workers alike report that where a child has behavioural problems a home broken or at risk of breakdown is the factor that features in the story more frequently than any other.[8]

As probation officers investigate offenders' backgrounds and make their report to judges before sentence is passed, they are in a good position to see the common causes underlying crime. One of these officers reported to me,

> Most of the trouble goes back to the home, with a history of disruption and violence. The common factor is the absence of the father. When a third person comes into the house, there is a feeling of hopelessness and a cycle of failure. The young person sees no purpose in trying, and is frightened to set goals. Often this leads to a life of sexual promiscuity.

I also interviewed a female police officer working among juveniles together with a Maori officer from the Justice Section of the Department of Social Welfare. Both agreed in making this statement:

> The majority of young people we meet come from broken homes. There is a common pattern of rebellion among kids who do not know who their natural parents are. This is more common among children who are not assimilated into an extended family.

THE CONTRAST

Many churches, church people, and other men and women of goodwill have been to the fore in showing compassion by offering advice and practical help. However, as with state agencies, much of their effort seems to be directed towards ameliorating the effects of wrongful actions rather than discerning and tackling the causes of trouble. A recent study of social issues states, 'As with many other major problems we face, New Zealand spends a fortune dealing with the results, and often spends very little on the cause.'[9] For instance, little is said by the helping professions and agencies to discourage sex outside of marriage, or to encourage those who have not practised it to continue abstaining. Instead they emphaisise 'safe sex' and the use of contraceptives, with a view to preventing disease and unwanted pregnancies. Little consideration is given to the psychological results of promiscuous sexual relationships or the lack of trust that often precedes and follows them.

The churches, as I indicated earlier, must bear some responsibility. The prophetic voice that should speak to church and nation is silent or muted regarding the importance of policies that will preserve and enhance the home as an integral part of society, and regarding the dangers attendant on its decline. I have tried to illustrate the truth of the apostolic teaching that when people turn their backs upon God, there is a sense in which—while his love and compassion never fail—he turns his back upon them. This is most eloquently expressed in the apostle Paul's letter to the Romans. This is a part of the Bible that at least as much as any part of Scripture shows the good news of the love of God in Jesus Christ. Yet the apostle begins by saying that men and women have turned aside from the knowledge of God that was open to them. 'They did not honour him as God or give thanks to him', but chose their own ways and made their own idols. So Paul repeats the solemn statement, 'God gave them up . . . God gave them up . . . God gave them up to a debased mind and to things that should not be done' (Romans 1:21-28). The awesome reality is that God leaves people to the consequences of their actions, until they turn back to him in repentance and faith.

Churches, I believe, have a positive message to offer a country whose families are being torn apart, and whose children flounder in a morass of bewilderment and hopelessness. They can point to families where God is honoured and where children are loved and given firm guidelines for living. There is still a message of grace and of vital relevance in the words of the Lord as recorded by the chronicler of Israel,

'If my people who are called by my name humble themselves, pray, seek my face, and turn from their wicked ways, then I will hear from heaven and forgive their sin and heal their land' (2 Chronicles 7:14).

NOTES

1. *Issues in human sexuality*, p.19.
2. Colossians 3:21; see also Ephesians 6:4.
3. See Exodus 12:24–27, 13:8-10 and 14, Deuteronomy 6:20–25, Joshua 4:4–7 and 21-24, and Psalm 78:1–8.
4. *Family matters No. 30*, Australian Institute of Family Studies, December 1991, p.50.
5. *Monthly summary of statistics Australia, June 1992*, Australian Bureau of Statistics.
6. *Pacific Network February 1992*, p.20, Pacific Foundation for Health, Education and Parent Support.
7. *Report of Ministerial Committee into Violence*, chaired by Sir Clinton Roper, 1987, p.95.
8. *Issues in human sexuality*, pp. 21–22

9. *Pacific Network February* 1992 (quoted above), p.29.

◆ CHAPTER 4 ◆

Sexuality and marriage

JOHN AND AGNES STURT

The second chapter of this book dealt with the way that Genesis 1 speaks of men and women created equally in the 'image of God'. In Genesis 2:24 God lays down the pattern for marriage and sexual expression within it. There marriage is defined by the *three statements*: 'a man will leave his father and mother and be united to his wife, and they will become one flesh' (NIV).

1. LEAVING

This means, first, a *physical* leaving. It is ideal for both the husband and wife to leave home to embark on their new relationship independently. This may be very difficult in some cultures and situations. Yet for both the man and the woman to pour their energies into their new relationship, they at least need to leave the authority and control of their parents. This involves an *emotional* leaving. They need to leave behind the pattern or model of marriage that they have both observed while growing up in order to decide what is right for them in their new relationship. Leaving implies a total commitment to the marriage and to the 'one flesh' relationship, from which all others are excluded.

The command to 'leave father and mother' is specifically addressed to the man. (The Hebrew word used here is *ish*, meaning a male, not *adam*, the generic term including both man and woman.) This is not to say that the woman should not also leave her home emotionally and physically; but it is especially important for the man to do so. In most cultures, however, until now it has been the woman who leaves home. A classic biblical example is the story of Isaac and Rebecca (Genesis 24). Rebecca made her decision to leave home, without even a farewell party. Isaac was 40 but it appears he never really left home, physically or emotionally. In fact, we are told that he brought Rebecca 'into his mother's tent', and this helped him cope with his mother's death. Hardly a good start for a marriage! Judging by the rest of the story, they certainly had problems becoming one in their attitude to their children.

2. CLEAVING

This is the word used in the older English translations, and it implies true bonding, with good communication and a uniting together emotionally. When it takes place, a good sexual relationship is possible. When it does not, sexual satisfaction in a long-term relationship is unlikely. Sexual enjoyment in marriage is intended to get better as time goes by. (The original Hebrew of Genesis 2:24 indicates a future 'they will become one'.) This sexual relationship between two people is an art to be learned, and it is unlikely to be fully satisfying until they really know one another. Like a good wine, sex should get better with age! Growth in emotional 'cleaving' enhances growth in sexual enjoyment. In turn, sexual enrichment enhances the intimacy of the relationship.

Emotional intercourse and sexual intercourse build on each other to ensure a mutually satisfying sexual experience.

3. BECOMING ONE

This is the goal of marriage. Becoming one includes sexual expression but it means much more. Some scholars point out that the Hebrew concept of becoming one involves the idea of 'weaving'. God's plan is for a man and a woman to weave their lives together emotionally, spiritually and physically. The sexual relationship is clearly a very important part of the marrying process and is intended to encourage and strengthen the weaving together of two lives. It is significant, however, that the sexual consummation of the relationship ('becoming one flesh') is the third step in the process of marrying. The two prior steps of leaving and cleaving are essential for a good sexual relationship to develop.

Bill and Susan's story illustrates this principle. They explained to their marriage counsellor that they had a sex problem. Susan never felt sexually fulfilled and seldom experienced an orgasm, while Bill felt very frustrated by Susan's lack of interest in sex. Their way of trying to deal with the problem was for Susan to go to bed early while Bill watched late shows on television. Naturally this led to a lot of coldness and arguments during the day.

As they explored their backgrounds with the counsellor, the couple realised that neither of their parents had modelled good communication. Susan's parents mainly related in a negative way by quarrelling and dumping their feelings on each other; they eventually separated. In contrast, Bill's parents stayed together, but never showed affection or shared their feelings in front of him. His father was a very private person. Susan and Bill had determined that they would not be like their parents, but, without realising it they had brought these poor communicating patterns with them into their own relationship. Neither of them had 'left' the marriage models they had seen.

Bill had fallen into the common pattern of trying to be married and single at the same time. He saw marriage as adding an asset to his life: a companion, housekeeper and sexual partner; but he had no intention of making any adjustments to his busy working and sporting schedule. He had not realised that it took time to build a relationship and that this involved sharing at a feeling level.

Eventually, Bill and Susan came to see what was going on in their marriage. They realised that if they were not communicating in the living room they would not have much success in the bedroom. They began learning to share their feelings and to be open and real with one another. They discovered that people, not just bodies, make love. They both needed more factual information about male and female sexual responses and the differences between them, but the main thing they learned was how to share at an emotional level. Old patterns die slowly, and Susan and Bill took some time to make changes, but gradually they developed a rewarding and satisfying emotional life, and with it came joy in their sexuality.

The relationship between the emotional and physical side of sexual intercourse is brought out by the language used in the Bible. It is significant that in Scripture the word for sexual intercourse in marriage is the word 'know', in the Hebrew, *yada* and in the Greek *ginosko*.[1] The Greek word in particular means not just a casual knowing but understanding completely, or knowing thoroughly. Sexual intercourse is intended to enhance the true knowing of one another that a man and a woman can experience in the intimacy and security of marriage.

SEX OUTSIDE MARRIAGE

The primary purpose of sexual expression

is *to promote the oneness of marriage* by enabling a man and a woman to 'know' each other fully, in a way that they do not know others. Sexual intercourse is intended for the exclusiveness of marriage.[2] The prohibition of sexual intercourse outside marriage is intended by God, our Creator, not to spoil our enjoyment of life but to enhance it. Sex within marriage builds and enriches, while outside marriage it destroys and debases. 'The adulteress preys upon your very life. Can a man scoop fire into his lap without his clothes being burned?' (Proverbs 6:26-27 NIV). 'All other sins a man commits are outside his body, but he who sins sexually sins against his own body' (1 Corinthians 6:18 NIV).

Within marriage sexual intercourse produces a rich bonding. There is also, however, a bonding that takes place when sex occurs outside marriage. St Paul says: 'Do you not know that whoever is united to a prostitute becomes one body with her? For it is said, 'The two shall be one flesh' (1 Corinthians 6:16). This other bonding causes confusion and the more it happens the more confusion occurs. Where there have been sexual liaisons before marriage, or extra-marital sex after marriage, these extra bondings, even if renounced, make it harder for the couple to 'become one' within their marriage. The philosophy of 'Try before you buy', or 'Sexual experience and experimentation before marriage makes sexual adjustment easier afterwards', is one of the adversary's lies.

Repentance and specific prayer are needed to break these confusing bonds. Through such confession and prayer the Lord will heal the hurts of the past and break the bonds that limit the enjoyment of his best for us. Forgiveness and freedom are possible, as Steven's story shows.[3]

Steven, a strong and active Christian, succumbed to temptation in a moment of weakness and committed adultery. His wife never found out and the extra-marital affair was totally ended. But Steven and Jo lost the joy and richness of their sexual relationship. Steven shared his situation with a mature Christian friend and confessed his sin to the Lord. His friend prayed with him for God to break the bond that the act of sex had established between him and the other woman. As a result, Steven and Jo grew into a new closeness in their marriage, and their sexual life regained its former beauty.

COHABITATION

In the Western world, living together before marriage has become a common practice. One person has described cohabitation as 'a bit like membership of a club or gym. You try it out for a while, and if it is a hit, you become a life member.'[4] Gary Jenkins, writing his excellent little book, *Cohabitation: a biblical perspective*, found in a survey of English parishes that 'Forty to 80 per cent of all couples who came to the church for a wedding were already living together.'[5] Many drift into this kind of relationship in a casual way, some for financial reasons, others because they are not legally free to marry. Some see it in terms of 'trial marriage', even as a substitute for marriage.

Reasons given for choosing this life-style often relate to fear of the commitment that is associated with marriage. Couples want the emotional and sexual closeness of marriage without losing the autonomy of singleness. The absence of long-term commitment is seen as a freedom that allows one or both of the partners to change their minds and leave the relationship, without the inconvenience of divorce.

Those who live together to test out their compatibility before deciding to marry are often disappointed. In talking to such couples, we have heard many of them report that their problems do not really emerge until after they marry. It has been estimated that when cohabiting couples marry, more than half of the resulting marriages fail. This is probably due to the fact that the insecurity of the situation when living together makes them more careful with one another, whereas after marriage it is easy to take one another for granted. Another significant fact is that most people, once they marry, consciously or unconsciously 'act married' in the way they saw their parents' marriage. Thus they bring to their own relationship two conflicting models of marriage, which were not there while they were living together. They need to acknowledge this, and to negotiate a new marriage pattern that is appropriate for them.

The Bible does not directly address the issue of cohabitation, nor does it lay down any formula for a marriage ceremony. It does however give clear guidelines for the marriage relationship. In contrast to most situations of cohabitation, the features of marriage according to the biblical model are these:

1. Permanence

We have seen that 'leaving' implies total commitment to the new relationship. This provides a secure foundation on which a strong marriage can be built, as opposed to the impermanence that a cohabitation arrangement usually involves.

2. Love

The Bible defines the quality of love expected in marriage as unconditional, self-giving, *agape* love, based on what we know of the way God loves us. While it is true that in many marriages love falls far short of this ideal, a committed marriage relationship provides the opportunity for this love to grow. In contrast, most cohabitation relationships are based essentially on mutual self-interest. That is, each partner is prepared to stay within the relationship providing their needs are being met. Phypers comments:

> Married love is sacrificial. It gives everything, even life itself, for the benefit and well-being of the spouse, but live-in love is selfish. It satisfies me now, and, when it fails, I can find someone else.[6]

3. Relationship

The concept of permanence implies also a quality of relationship as well as quantity. It is true that some live-in relationships are of high quality and may be long-lasting. Casual cohabitation situations, however, do not usually have the ideal of excellence that is built in to the covenant of marriage as expressed in a Christian marriage service.

4. Community dimension

Cohabitation is a private affair. Marriage, on the other hand, involves a relationship, not only between two people but also two families. It has the recognition and support of the community; and in the case of Christian marriage, of the Church. It is publicly sealed by covenant vows before God, family and friends. When the couple takes these vows seriously, it adds stability and strength to the union.

5. Security for children

Children need the security of two parents committed to loving each other, and them, on a permanent basis. This is part of the purpose of marriage, and it is often recognised by couples living together when they decide to have children. It is understandable that at this point many decide to marry.

6. Sex

We have already seen that the Bible links sex with the idea of 'becoming one'. (Genesis 2:24). Smedes argues that because sexual union is a 'life-uniting act, to engage in a life-uniting act without a life-uniting intent' is to miss its true purpose.[7] It is often argued that a 'trial marriage' is a sensible step by which two people can discover if they are compatible. In fact it is a using of one another; and it falls far short of the biblical ideal of sex as part of a growing experience of 'becoming one', possible when two people are fully committed to each other's welfare.

MUTUALITY OF SEX IN MARRIAGE

God created man and woman as *equal partners* in marriage so that they might together reflect his image (Genesis 1:27). However, this relationship deteriorated after the Fall. In Genesis 3:16 we read that God said to the woman: 'Your desire shall be for your husband, and he shall rule over you.' This was not God's original plan for them, but the consequence of their sin. The word 'desire' is the Hebrew word *teshuqah*, which does not mean here a longing for the husband, but a desire to rule over him. (The next time it is used is in Genesis 4:7, which demonstrates the emphasis of this word. Here God is talking to Cain and says sin's 'desire is for you, but you must master it'.) Thus the battle of the sexes started and is still with us today. Man, who was the stronger physically, gained the upper hand. In most cultures, sexual inequality is represented by male domination.

One of the most destructive ways in

which this domination is expressed is in sexual oppression and even abuse. The power struggle between men and women can be expressed most bitterly through our sexuality. This can happen in Christian marriages, where the wife has been wrongly taught that it is her duty to submit sexually, and that the sex act is at her husband's desire and control.

God's answer to this inequality and conflict is in the cross. Jesus came not only to bring salvation but reconciliation: between humanity and God, between man and woman, between one person and another. 'For he is our peace; in his flesh he has made both groups into one and has broken down the dividing wall, that is, the hostility between us' (Ephesians 2:14). Barriers to becoming one have been broken down through Christ's death on the cross; whether barriers of race (as in the context of this passage), status or sex. (See also Galatians 3:28.)

A key to Christian marriage is identified in Ephesians 5:21: 'Be subject to one another out of reverence for Christ.' Christian marriage is a relationship of mutual submission and mutual servanthood because Christ is the head of this relationship. This mutual submission must be expressed in the couple's sexual relationship as in every other aspect of their partnership. Paul takes this up in writing to the Corinthians about marriage. 'The husband should fulfill his marital duty to his wife, and likewise the wife to her husband. The wife's body does not belong to her alone but also to her husband. In the same way the husband's body does not belong to him alone but also to his wife' (1 Corinthians 7:3-4 NIV).

Another emphasis in Ephesians 5 is the supreme importance of love. Of course, love is to be expressed by both partners, but here specifically husbands are told: 'Love your wives, just as Christ loved the church and gave himself up for her' (verse 25). Thus they are not merely told to love their wives, but how to love: it must be sacrificial love, patterned on Jesus himself.

The linking of the teaching in Ephesians 5 with that in 1 Corinthians 7 shows clearly that one spouse does not have unlimited sexual access to the other. In Ephesians 5:28-29 the teaching is that because his wife's body belongs to him, the husband has the responsibility to care for and nurture it, meeting his wife's needs and considering her wishes. The reverse is also true. In the 1 Corinthians 7 context Paul says: 'Do not deprive one another except perhaps by agreement and for a set time . . .' This attitude removes the battle from the bedroom, and sets the stage for a mutually satisfying sexual relationship.

In summary we may say that good sex requires three essentials: healthy attitudes, adequate information, and good communication.

Many people bring into marriage wrong or negative *attitudes* to sex, picked up from their family or cultural environment. Unless these are challenged and changed they will sabotage the freedom and joy that couples might have in their sexual expression. When these negative attitudes to sex are combined with lack of *information* or misinformation about human sexual response, the result can be disastrous. These were problems that Bill and Susan started with, but they did not have the skills even to talk about them.

Good communication is the basis for learning how to share sexually; without this skill there are sure to be problems. Sexual intercourse involves communication at all levels: physical, emotional, intellectual and spiritual. A communication breakdown in one or more of these areas will upset the process. The essence of good communication is described succinctly in Ephesians 4:15 as 'speaking the truth in love'. Paul adds that this is the way to 'grow up'. (The context here refers to spiritual growth into Christ, but what is said is true of any encounter between persons.) In sexual intercourse the 'truth' is how I really feel about myself and my partner, but this has to be communicated in a loving way. Skilful communication leads to a level of intimacy in which physical sexual expression flows naturally.

The basic text that we have considered in Genesis 2:24 calls us to be aware of three problems that occur often in sexual relationships:

- One or both partners have not 'left' unhealthy sexual attitudes or misinformation which they picked up in their childhood about sex.

- They have not learned how to 'cleave' to one another in good and open communication.

- Consequently they are blocked in their experience of 'becoming one', sexually, as well as in other aspects of intimacy.

THE PURPOSES OF SEX IN MARRIAGE

The Bible affirms that there are four purposes for sex in marriage: procreation, protection, pleasure and the promotion of oneness.

1. Procreation

The first command given in scripture is: 'Be fruitful and multiply' (Genesis 1:28). It is virtually the only command of God that humankind has taken seriously! But let us be sensitive to the fact that about 11 per cent of couples are unable to have children for one reason or another. While childlessness is sad for the couple, a marriage is nevertheless complete without children. There is no mention of children in the basic statement on marriage in Genesis 2:24. In fact, in Scripture children are not usually referred to in the same context as instruction about sex. Children are not the marriage; they are a gift and blessing from God.[8]

Every child should be a wanted child. For the Christian couple this means that the decision to have children should be a matter for prayer and guidance. The main purpose of sex in marriage is to enhance the oneness of the relationship, not merely to have children. Thus, contraception becomes a responsible act that couples have to work out together.

2. Protection

In the very practical passage about sex that we have already referred to (1 Corinthians 7:1-7), Paul points out that marriage provides a proper safeguard against the immorality of the world around and a healthy way of helping people maintain sexual self-control. That safeguard is certainly present when the sexual relationship is mutually satisfying and fulfilling.

3. Pleasure

One whole book in the Bible, The Song of Songs, is devoted to a detailed description of married love and the joy and pleasure which can be found in the 'one flesh' relationship. Many have treated this book as a beautiful allegory of the relationship between Christ and his bride, the Church. But primarily it is a love song describing the courtship, marriage, wedding night and subsequent sexual adjustments between the bridegroom (traditionally considered to be Solomon) and his country bride. The book is poetry, set in an ancient Hebrew context, so it is helpful to use a good commentary to understand it.[9]

The song depicts a balance and equality in the couple's relationship and in their love-making. Both partners take the initiative and both respond to the advances of the other. They are friends as well as lovers (5:1, 16). There is a clear progression in their relationship. The bride begins with a possessive statement: 'My beloved is mine and I am his' (2:16) i.e. 'I've got him!' As their love grows, she says: 'I am my beloved's and my beloved is mine' (6:3). Finally she expresses a mature understanding: 'I belong to my beloved and his desire is for me' (7:10).

The sexual consummation of their marriage is described beautifully and symbolically in 4:16 as the bride invites her husband to come and enjoy his garden, which he does (5:1). Then follows a profound instruction: 'Eat, O friends, drink; and drink your fill, O lovers' (NIV). This is the central statement of the song, telling us plainly that God views sex in marriage as a blessing to be richly enjoyed.

The expression of our sexuality is important not just for the start of marriage. Proverbs 5:15-23 is a passage well worth studying, as it emphasises that sexual intercourse is to be kept for marriage and is 'not for sharing with strangers'. But it continues: 'rejoice in the wife of your youth', not merely in your youth and hers! 'May you be intoxicated always by her love'. Sexual intercourse is intended to enrich the whole of life; in fact, it should get better as the years go by.

4. Promoting oneness

As we have seen above, this is the chief purpose of the gift of sex in marriage, to enable husband and wife to 'know' each other more and to grow in their intimacy. Sex is intended to be the uninhibited gift to each other of who we are.

Mary and Tony brought to their marriage a deep love and a strong Christian faith, but they also brought with them negative sexual attitudes. Tony's parents had not told him anything about sex, from which he deduced that keen Christians should not be interested in it. Mary came with an even more negative concept that 'sex was dirty'. They had not received any positive teaching on marriage in their church.

Their honeymoon was a disappointment to both of them as far as its sexual expression was concerned. Things did not get any better in the next few years. The arrival of two children in fairly quick succession, bringing disturbed sleep and many demands, did not help. After they had been married five years they sought counselling, thoroughly disillusioned and feeling somewhat hopeless about their situation. Their love and commitment to the marriage, however, gave them the strength to work on their problems.

They were helped to challenge and change the negative attitudes that they had grown up with. As they made a more careful study of the relevant passages in Scripture on the subject of sex in marriage their eyes were opened. They were also given some specific and accurate information about the functioning of their bodies and about human sexual response, and were directed to a good book on the subject.

They learned how to share feelings, something which had been missing from their communication. They would spend up to half an hour a day sharing at this deeper level. They could now talk about their sexual experiences together, telling each other what their needs were. Their doctor helped them to find a more satisfactory method of contraception. At the end of four months Mary experienced an orgasm for the first time. Bed ceased to be a battle-ground and became a place where they could enjoy each other, not only physically but emotionally. Their new level of communication provided the tools to deal with other problems in their relationship.

CONCLUSION

We can only conclude in wonder and gratitude for the wisdom of the Bible, God's word. It is truly the 'Handbook of the Maker's Instructions', providing us with specific information about the purposes of our sexuality and clear guidance for sex in marriage. The Scriptures teach and encourage the joyous expression of our sexuality in

marriage to the end that we may truly
become one.

NOTES

1. For example, see Genesis 4:1 and Matthew 1:25.
2. See Exodus 20:14, Proverbs 5:15-18, 1 Thessalonians 4:3-4 and Hebrews 13:4.
3. 1 John 1:9 and James 5:16.
4. *Daily Mirror*, 17 April 1989 (London), p. 17.
5. Gary Jenkins, *Cohabitation: A biblical perspective* (Grove Books,1992). We gratefully acknowledge our use, in this section, of insights drawn from this book.
6. D Phypers, *Christian marriage in crisis* (MARC, 1985) p.72.
7. Lewis Smedes, *Sex in the real world* (Lion, 1976), p.122.
8. See Genesis 12:2, 17:6 and Psalm 127:3-5.
9. Craig Glickman, *A song for lovers* (Inter-Varsity Press, 1976) and Joseph Dillow, *Solomon on sex* (Thomas Nelson,1977).

RECOMMENDED READING

Arnold Fruchtenbaum, *Biblical lovemaking* (Ariel Press).

Dennis Guernsey, *Thoroughly married* (Key Word, 1981).

Joyce Huggett, *Growing into love* (Inter-Varsity Press, 1982).

Joyce Huggett, *Life in a sex-mad society* (Inter-Varsity Press, 1988).

Morton and Barbara Kelsey, *Sacrament of sexuality* (Amity House, 1986).

R. Meier, L. Meier, S. Minirth and P. Meier, *Sex in the Christian marriage* (Baker, 1988).

Herbert Miles, *Sexual happiness in marriage* (Zondervan, 1967).

Clifford and Joyce Penner, *A gift for all ages* (Word, 1986).

Clifford and Joyce Penner, *The gift of sex* (Word, 1981).

Philip Rice, *Sexual problems in marriage* (Westminster, 1978).

Letha Scanzoni, *Sex is a parent affair* (Regal, 1973).

Ed and Gaye Wheat, *Intended for pleasure* (Revell, 1977).

◆ CHAPTER 5 ◆

The single life

PETER LINEHAM

In Western societies today there are nearly as many single adults as there are married couples. If the church wants to touch people's needs, it must be able to speak clearly to the needs and pressures of singleness. That is the challenge this chapter seeks to address.

CHURCHES AND SINGLENESS

In the life of the churches single people often feel that they are regarded as immature and incomplete. They are expected to volunteer for various subordinate tasks, while married people may cite family responsibilities and be excused.

Such an approach to singles is plainly inappropriate. But what pattern should the church adopt? Singles today often seek out churches that provide activities and groups just for them (although childless married couples often want the same). Many of these singles are separated or divorced, while others are widows and widowers, who may live many years after the death of their spouse. In American churches ministries to single people have flourished, but often quite separately from other church activities.

THE SACRED PROTESTANT FAMILY

Many Christian married couples feel threatened by the increasing number of single people in society and the church. Yet they have forgotten the heritage of the church over many centuries: the celibate priesthood and the orders. The protestant churches in the sixteenth century rejected that heritage and so gave marriage a unique status. Of course in days gone by the family was an economic as well as a social unit. Families worked together and provided a form of social security for each other. As a result of the economic and social changes of the past two centuries, people's work has become separated from their home and family. The family is now less important as an economic unit, and thus singleness has become economically viable.

Churches have rallied to the defence of the family, and many churches emphasise ministry to families. Churches call themselves 'family' churches, and the word 'family' is given special Christian significance. A church obviously ought to advise and help parents to bring up their children in a Christian way, and to encourage husbands and wives in their married relationship. However, this is only one of the many social responsibilities of the church, and after all it may be that only a minority of today's church members are in nuclear families. The Bible does not regard the nuclear family as sacred. Jesus recognised that family pressures could be an obstacle to the gospel, and he said: 'Whoever comes to me and does not hate father and mother . . . cannot be my disciple' (Luke 14:26). God alone is sacred; all other social institutions have a lesser role.[1] While ministry to families is important, it must not be the church's exclusive contribution to social life.

THE CHOICE OF SINGLENESS OR MARRIAGE

In the age of the early church, marriages were arranged for most young people while they were growing up. Jesus by his own example, however, gave a new dignity to singleness. The apostle Paul also made a strong case for singleness in 1 Corinthians 7, though his argument was based on the crisis conditions which Christianity then faced.

Singleness and marriage should not be viewed as in being competition. Single people as well as those who are married need to understand the biblical view of marriage as a part of God's purpose that reflects his creating and restoring work in the world. The biblical teaching of 'one flesh', the physical and spiritual unity of husband and wife, insists that it is a special fulfilment of God's creative purposes, and the God-given context for children to be conceived, born, and brought up.

EVERYONE IS SINGLE FOR A WHILE

While married people need to understand the significance of marriage, they must equally understand the value of singleness. Both conditions have a place in God's purposes. We all start off as single people. Some adults are single only until they are married;

some are single because they cannot find a partner. Others will return to singleness because they have lost a partner through divorce or death. Others choose singleness on a longer-term basis. Consequently all need to learn how to be happily single.

I wish that everyone who got married understood what they were doing. So many people, including Christians, get married because they are in love with love, and because they are so poor at being single. They seek a partner to support them because they are insecure about themselves. Those who get married because they are lonely or unhappy will find themselves in difficulties because they expect too much from their marriage partner. Such marriages are inward-looking love-nests, whereas marriage should create a relationship to be shared with others from a position of security. People are only ready to be married when they know how to be single. Even those for whom singleness is simply a short-term passage in which they prepare for marriage need to be careful.

The skills that singleness develops are not incompatible with marriage. Those who cannot manage to care for themselves, and who view their partner as the equivalent of their mother or father, are ignoring the biblical vision of married life.

Those who remain single into their thirties and beyond must, I think, come to a point of real acceptance of their situation, and indeed make a positive commitment to it. Otherwise they will feel bitter or self-pitying, or be pained by every passing comment; or they will find themselves in a state of desperation, inclined to leap at any hope of happiness, however unsuitable or unwise, be it a change of job, church or place of residence, or to respond to a marriage offer from someone quite incompatible with them. Positive commitment does not mean a lifelong vow—such vows are generally unwise. God may use singleness at one stage in a person's life and marriage at another stage. I do not need to be self-conscious about my singleness; nevertheless I need to be aware of its implications.

SINGLENESS AND SEX

Single people often struggle to exercise sexual self-control. In Paul's day arranged marriages at a younger age reduced some of these problems. In our age few people are virgins when they get married. In society generally, virginity is most frequently lost in the teens, while marriage takes place in the mid to late twenties. Because marriage is often long delayed, in Christian circles as well as elsewhere, some single people are simply following popular custom in 'seeing the world before they tie themselves down'. Given this motivation, and the prevailing emphasis on sexual 'liberation', singleness has real pressures. Yet the Bible's teaching is clear that sexual purity is God's requirement for single people. Paul in 1 Corinthians 7 instructs those unable to control their sexual passions that it is better to marry than to 'burn' with sexual desire. It is not a Christian option for a single person to sleep around.

Single people, however, are still feeling, loving, sexual beings. They can be made to feel that they are missing true fulfilment, and that the sex act is the only way to express love. Single people certainly must be able to control their sexual feelings; but that does not mean that they have no feelings. Everyone is vulnerable, and the media can stimulate private fantasies of sexual achievement that may leave people very unhappy. Masturbation is not just an issue for single people, and its significance can be exaggerated. Nevertheless single people must avoid using it as a substitute for other sexual activity, for it indicates sexual desires out of control.

I believe that we single people can learn restraint while recognising our sexual character. These words apply equally to those who experience homosexual desires as they do to heterosexual people. Above all, single people need to mature in all their relationships, so that they are able to give and express warmth and love.

THE SINGLE PERSON NEEDS FRIENDS

We need to recover the concept of friendship. Christians, like the rest of society, are not good at it. Yet one of the great joys of life is friendship at a deep level. The single person can find the emotional support from friendship that others find in marriage. After all, the unity in marriage is far more a matter of emotional than physical commitment; it is a caring relationship.

The friend also makes a commitment. The beautiful biblical example of the friendship of David and Jonathan was based upon a covenant. Their friendship was not politically expedient; each risked himself by being open with the other. Jesus gives the highest example of what a friend should be, as he was regarded by others as the 'friend of tax collectors and sinners' (Matthew 11:19).

In some societies like mine in New Zealand, males are supposed to be 'mates', yet they are not supposed to show their warm feelings. Friendship between men can, however, be a very special bond, even if they are arguably less self-aware than women and more likely to concentrate on shared interests than on understanding and strengthening one another. For single males such links can be important, although I would emphasise equally the importance of friendship with females and with couples. We need friends from the other sex. Jesus was friendly with Mary and Martha. Friendship with the other sex keeps us from the worst characteristics of the unkempt male, broadens our outlook on life and keeps us from having stereotyped or distorted ideas about them, or from feeling self-conscious in their presence.

Admittedly friendships with the other sex can have complications, for not everyone is single for the same reason. Some men and women seeking marriage partners will be obliged to remain single. Many of us might have married in different circumstances. Ideally we will all be able to accept our singleness, but it is more difficult for some than others. Some never give up the hope of marriage and view every single person of the opposite sex as a potential partner. This problem affects both men and women, but in modern western society there are significantly more women than men, and in the church the disproportion of women is even greater.

I was once rather naive about the possibility of such signals from the other sex; but I have learned that such naivety is not excusable, and that, if not anticipated, it can ruin relationships. We need to be realistic that problems like this can happen, and we need to be aware of our own suppressed intentions. Men, when outnumbered by women, need to be careful not to abuse their position, and should be aware that signals of friendship are sometimes misinterpreted. Happily, most friendships across the sexes are not like this.

THE CHRISTIAN COMMUNITY AND SINGLE PEOPLE

Many single people suffer from isolation, and this seems to make a few of them vulnerable to neuroses, depression, and even the classic eccentricities of the bachelor! To become bitter in one's isolation, to develop one's own peculiar and anti-social mode of life is neither sensible nor rewarding, but it is possible for those people who have been widowed or who feel 'left on the shelf'.

The people of God have an answer to

such feelings. In Psalm 68:5-6 (NIV) God is described as 'a father to the fatherless, a defender of widows' who 'sets the lonely in families'. Christians should find their security in God himself, and, no matter what their background, they all should experience the family life of the people of God. The Bible uses the image of family about the church because Christians have a commitment which does not arise from feelings of affinity. We are in the Christian family to support one another, no matter how different we are.

For this reason singleness should not have to mean living alone. In 1 Timothy, 5 Paul indicates that widows who were not going to be remarried were enrolled in a special order so they could become a community supporting one another. Churches which have failed to develop and use communities have missed out on significant resources. It is time for us to re-create committed communities for people to belong to either on a short term or a long term basis. Such communities can include married couples as well as singles—although each need their own security of identity and private space if the community is to last. Such communities also offer a way to support the old and the handicapped; and they enable single people to be less wasteful of resources, which then are available for the kingdom of God. The church is an ideal body to provide the equivalent of a family for those who need it.

MAKING A SUCCESS OF SINGLENESS

I have come to the conclusion that singleness need not be a synonym for misery, and gradually I have learned that there can be real fulfilment in it. I meet plenty of people, however, who have not yet found their way out of the problems of singleness. I believe that we will gain hope and direction when we recognise that we have an ability to help ourselves by the grace of God. It is when I start putting effort into relationships that they begin to grow, and although this can be hard work, I honestly believe that we must not just blame our problems on others. Anybody who wants to can grow through involvement with others. The biblical exhortation to show hospitality is not directed only to married people; the single person should act like a whole person, even if some people treat him or her as incomplete.

There is a risk in this advice. We single people need to be careful that we do not volunteer for tasks in order to receive affirmation of our usefulness and our maturity from other (especially married) people. We need a private world too. We must ensure that our contentment is internal and is not derived from our activity. We need to know how to enjoy ourselves and to feel contented.

This generally means learning about being contented on our own. There is a real phobia of loneliness in our society. Loneliness brings pressure, of course, which can strike us down mercilessly when we least expect it, but if we have come to terms with who we are and how the Lord is with us, we need never feel utterly alone. Instead we have the great privilege of space, for which many married people feel a desperate need.

The greatest privilege of those of us who are single is being able to choose and enjoy things for and by ourselves. In fact singleness has huge advantages—so great that there are strong temptations to be single in order to live a comfortable and selfish life. I admit that this can be a motive for singleness, although self-indulgence is a sad and empty choice. Some people talk about the importance of 'loving yourself'. This is a serious distortion of biblical truth and a trap for single people. We do need self-knowledge, but it should be a path to unselfishness and unself-consciousness, not self-love. We need Christian motives for the whole of life.

SINGLENESS AND THE KINGDOM OF GOD

All of us, single and married, should live lives dedicated to the Lord. We are all called to serve the kingdom of God. 1 Corinthians 7:25-35 teaches that singleness for the Christian should not be an excuse for self-indulgence, but an opportunity for uninterrupted service of God. In contrast, the married person has entered a permanent commitment to his or her family. Marriage is a calling to two people to find unity of purpose towards each other and their family. As a result married people have very limited choices in certain issues. They are not as free to serve the Lord; they must do so in the context of spouse and family. Singles, in contrast, should delight in the opportunities they have. If they choose, they have the freedom to get up and go when someone is needed, to move quickly in response to particular needs. The single person is free, but it is a freedom not to serve self but to serve God.

This approach is in sharp contrast to that of the world, which may see advantages in singleness. The Bible sees it as a state that can free us for the work of God. Jesus' comments about eunuchs in Matthew 19:12 suggest this. It may sound a raw deal, of course, if you are told that the Lord has left you single so that you can help others. Many single people have reason to complain about the pressure they are faced with to serve in the Sunday school, to babysit or do door-to-door visitation while married people plead family responsibilities as a reason for saying no. Such pressure is unfair, and church authorities ought to be more sensitive to each person and their gifts and needs. But don't waste the privilege that we have as single people. I possess what married people lack, the freedom to say 'yes', the freedom to serve God without hindrance from family responsibilities. For myself I don't particularly mind if the dishes pile up, or my house isn't very tidy, when there are more important things to do. Doubtless most singles are more house-proud than me, and serving the Lord should not be an excuse for irresponsibility or neglect of other aspects of life, but nevertheless, as single people we have opportunities to serve the Lord freely. It is great to see whole families serving God, but one member of the family must not conscript others unwillingly. For me as a single person there should be no hindrance in my relationships from following the Lord where he leads.

Jesus, the model single person

The Lord Jesus lived wholly for the will

of God. What a model he is for all of us! All of us, women and men, married and single, can identify with him, because he identified with us. He did not do his own will but the will of God. He was alone, but he was not lonely, because he experienced fellowship with God, and with those who followed him. If this was his experience, then singleness cannot be unblessed, and it need not be unproductive. We single people can follow his way of life (1 John 4:17), and that is surely a great privilege.

NOTE

1. See J A Walter, *A long way from home: a sociological exploration of contemporary idolatry* (Paternoster, 1979) pp. 47–66.

RECOMMENDED READING

Gini Andrews, *Your half of the apple* (Zondervan, 1972).

Barbara Sroka, *One is a whole number* (Victor Books, 1978).

◆ CHAPTER 6 ◆

Sexuality and singleness

SHEILA PRITCHARD

GIFT, CALL OR NECESSITY

There are many different kinds of single people. Some have never married; others are widowed, separated or divorced. Some have turned down opportunities of marriage while others have never had such opportunities. There are single people who have had, or are currently involved in, sexual relationships outside marriage, and those who are virgins. There are single people who long above all else for marriage, and those who

abhor the very idea. Some see their singleness as a special call of God, others as a cruel
curse. Every single person has a unique history and individual needs. But what all have
in common is a sexuality that is integral to
their very nature.

SEXUALITY AND THE NATURE OF GOD

There is more to sexuality than sexual
intercourse. Any single person wanting to
come to terms with sexuality must be clear
about this at the outset. Sexuality—all that it
means to be male or female—is built into
every aspect of our being. Thus the single
person, no less than the married person,
should embrace and celebrate God's gift of
sexuality.

Sexuality is not only God's gift, it is God's
way of demonstrating that femaleness and
maleness each express aspects of the divine
nature. This is made clear in Genesis 1:27. To
live fully one's womanhood or manhood is
to sense the wonder of being made in God's
image.

What does it mean for a single person to
live womanhood or manhood fully? Society
gives very strong messages that fullness of
life is not possible without sexual relationships, and many, if not most, single people

find this hard to refute. Does the Bible support the conviction that there can be fulfilment of life and celebration of sexuality for those who are celibate? Surely yes, consider Jesus!

Genital, biological and affective sexuality

To lay a foundation for this discussion we need to clarify some terminology. If sexuality includes all of our maleness or femaleness then genital sexual activity represents only a small part of the whole. This we shall call genital sexuality. When we speak of the biological differences which are inherent in our bodies, genes and chromosomes, we are talking about biological sexuality. Then there are the issues of intimacy: friendship, mutual support, shared ideas and companionship. These are aspects of our affective sexuality— the expression of our male/female personhood at the level of emotions and psyche.

These three aspects of sexuality cannot be rigidly compartmentalised; they all influence one another. Nevertheless they are not identical. To abstain from genital activity is not to diminish one's sexuality. In fact Jesus spoke of abstinence as one way of living fully for the kingdom of God (Matthew 19:12).

Jesus models celibate sexuality

Jesus models healthy sexuality at all levels. There was no question about his masculinity, or biological sexuality. He was brought up according to the appropriate cultural norms for Jewish males and was obviously a man whom other men respected. Jesus' life is also a rich demonstration of a person at home with his affective sexuality. He openly enjoyed the companionship of both men and women, gave and received touch to and from both, shared his ideas and his emotions with his close friends and didn't hesitate to express his need of their support. In other words, Jesus was not afraid of intimacy.

Jesus did not have a sexual partner. In the realm of genital sexuality he models abstinence. One of the key purposes of the incarnation is to show us what fulfilment of humanity means. The fulfilled humanity which Jesus lived out did not include genital sexual activity or marriage. This does not make genital sexual activity wrong or a second-best life-style, but it does mean that it is not essential to a fulfilling life.

Pondering the significance of the fullness of life modelled by Jesus ought to help to overcome the culturally reinforced notion of incompleteness that is often felt by single people. But we must face the reality that most single people are battling not only cultural messages, but also their own natural physical drives and desires. Our society's current attitude to such drives and desires is that the only 'healthy' thing to do is to find a sexual partner. Christians have been slow to show that there is an alternative that really satisfies the underlying longing.

SEXUALITY AND SPIRITUALITY

What is the underlying longing? This is a crucial question. At the heart of our nature as humans is the desire to be fully known and loved. God intended it this way. Our longings for intimacy and communion with one another are a constant reminder of the intimacy and communion inherent in God, the Trinity. At the very heart of human sexuality is a longing for union and communion with someone who, knowing us completely, will love us unconditionally.

The deepest and most profound experience of union and unconditional love is not to be found in genital sexuality. A single person who believes that ultimate satisfaction lies there suffers from tunnel vision which may obscure a deeper level of joyful wholeness. Both Jesus and Paul leave us in no doubt that both marriage and celibacy are lifestyles in which fulfilment can be found.[1] This is precisely because the ultimate source of satisfaction is to be found with the only partner who can ever know us completely and love us unconditionally—God.

A Christian marriage can point to some wonderful things about union with God through the joy of closely shared lives and sacrificial love for one another (Ephesians 5:22-33). A Christian celibate can also point to the reality of union with God through radical trust in his sufficiency and the joyful freedom of total availability.[2] Both lifestyles involve sacrifice; neither offers unmitigated utopia in this life!

In such ways we can see that sexuality and spirituality are integrally related. The longings for union, communion and creation of life that characterise sexuality, are also the hallmarks of spiritual desire. For me this is the key to living a celibate life with a true sense of fulfilment and purpose. I can enjoy being known and loved and supported in varying degrees by people whom God gives me as friends, but I expect no one to fill the space closest to my heart where only God satisfies. I will never bear children of my own, but I can be a co-creator with God in bringing life to others in a variety of ways.

YES, BUT . . .

No matter how willingly the celibate Christian embraces the perspectives outlined above, life as a single person is not free of pain. (Neither, of course, is life as a married person!) Some of the most commonly expressed problems are loneliness, identity, touch hunger and appropriate release of sexual tension.

Loneliness

There is no escape from the fact that at times it is intensely painful to realise there is no one special person for me. Loneliness at that level cannot be relieved merely by finding some people to socialise with, though taking initiatives to enjoy one's friends can prevent the loneliness deepening into self-pity. Perhaps the real issue is not so much relieving the pain as daring to enter it fully. When single people allow this particular Gethsemane to lead them to closer identification with Jesus, it leads them also to know him in a new way as an understanding Lover.

Identity

For some single people in our couple-oriented society, self-esteem and identity are undermined by lack of a partner. This ought not to be so, but sadly it is. It highlights the fact that we place more store in being chosen by another person than in being chosen by God. To be someone's sexual partner (whether married to them or not) is seen to give status and identity. To be chosen by God to live some part (or all) of life in partnership with him alone should surely be no less affirming.

Touch hunger

Someone has said that our skin is our largest sex organ. This is not meant to be either flippant or distasteful; touch is an extremely important expression of human caring and connectedness. Bearing in mind that sexuality encompasses far more than just genitality, touch is an essential ingredient in healthy celibate sexuality. Jesus frequently gave and received touch as an expression of love and healing. Yet many single people suffer from a 'touch hunger' which is as real as hunger for food. Unless the normal human need for loving touch is met in appropriate ways there is potential for it to become focussed genitally and then there may be a demand that is difficult to resist.

Sexual tension

To stress that sexuality is more than genitality is not in any way to deny that it is genital. Sexual arousal is a natural (and God created) response which single people experience too. If the whole range of one's sexuality is being continually integrated in some of the ways described above, such arousal need not create unmanageable tensions. Nevertheless, to experience a physical arousal that one chooses not to fulfil in sexual intercourse, does involve tension. Views on the acceptability of masturbation for the Christian vary widely. In the end the answer is probably neither an unqualified yes or no. Like many other things on which Scripture is silent a deeper question determines the answer. In this case the question might be: 'What is the best way, in this situation, to both channel and celebrate the energy of my God-given sexuality?'

Self-control is involved in channelling the energy of sexual arousal. But self-control should not be confused with denial or repression. Sexual energy is a welcome sign of health, and it is possible to choose to use that energy constructively. As with any other surge of energy caused by some stimulus (for example the energy of anger or of delight), a mature adult decides whether to express the energy physically or not, and if so, in what ways.

In other words, the physical release of sexual energy through masturbation may be an appropriate choice on some occasions. At other times a different physical activity, such as sport, other forms of exercise or even vigorous housework, is more appropriate. Others find creative activities such as writing, art or dance provide a satisfying outlet. In the lifetime of a single person, many of these alternatives will probably be useful at different times.

The deciding factor, in my view, is the question I raised above, which I think is worth repeating: 'What is the best way, in this situation, to both channel and celebrate the energy of my God given sexuality?' The key is to share both the tension and the choice for action with Jesus, who is not only my Lord but also the one who loves me most intimately.

INTEGRATED SEXUALITY FOR THE SINGLE CHRISTIAN

Integration of all aspects of one's sexuality is surely the key to living in joyful wholeness as a single Christian. Human beings are sexual beings; to deny that fact is to turn from God's offer of fullness of life (John 10:10). To accept the invitation involves acknowledging the particular richness of masculinity/femininity as it expresses God's nature. It involves celebrating the gifts of friendship, intimacy and relational connectedness even as Jesus did. It involves entering fully into our longings for union, communion and creation, and realising their ultimate fulfilment in oneness with Christ.[3] It involves addressing the tensions and difficulties of singleness wisely and willingly, recognising that, single or married, no human life is stress free.

Jesus, who esteemed marriage highly as expressing God's image (Matthew 19:4-5), was himself God in the form of a celibate male. What further proof do we need that sexuality and singleness can be integrated in lives lived fully in union with God?

NOTES
1. Matthew 19:1-12; 1 Corinthians 7:25-40; Ephesians 5:22-33.
2. 1 Corinthians 7:32-35; Matthew 19:12.
3. Colossians 2:9-10.

RECOMMENDED READING

Audrey Beslow, *Sex and the single Christian* (Abingdon,1987).

Julia Duin, *Sex and the single Christian* (Marshall Pickering, 1990).

Richard Foster, *Money, sex and power* (Hodder & Stoughton, 1985).

Donald Goergen, *The sexual celibate* (SPCK,1976).

Tim Stafford, *The sexual Christian* (Scripture Press, 1989).

♦ CHAPTER 7 ♦

How safe is safe sex?

NEIL D BROOM

History is punctuated with numerous technological discoveries that have revolutionised human affairs. We have had the Bronze Age, the Iron Age and the Age of Steam. Welcome now to the 'Age of the Condom'.

Just three decades ago came the discovery of the contraceptive pill—and with it an enormous change in sexual behaviour. It was the Golden Age of sexual liberation—the so-called swinging sixties. In a very brief space of time the age-old link between marriage, sexual intercourse and procreation was well and truly severed. Sex became primarily recreational thanks to the contraceptive pill's power to eliminate or control any unintended procreational consequences. This new found freedom from the fear of unintended pregnancy had the potential for opening the way to deeper levels of love and communication within marriage. (The appropriate use of contraception within marriage has been referred to in chapter 4.) Yet the same freedom also brought a staggering increase in pre-marital and extra-marital sexual activity.

THE REALITY OF SEXUALLY TRANSMITTED DISEASES

In the heat of this sexual revolution too little thought was given to the diseases that burgeoned in response to the increasingly complex web of casual sexual relationships. In the last three decades the number of sexually transmitted diseases of epidemiological importance has increased from five to more than twenty. Their long term consequences can be tragic in terms of physical and emotional suffering, and include primary infertility, ectopic or tubal pregnancy, stillbirth and early infant death, cancer and AIDS.[1]

SECURITY IN TECHNOLOGY OR IN MORALITY?

The radical shift in sexual values that I have referred to above must also be considered in the context of our western culture, which has been profoundly influenced by the brilliant successes of modern science. The sheer power of science to unlock many of nature's deepest secrets and to transform almost every aspect of our daily lives has given our society a very strong sense that science, and its applied arm, technology, will in the end get us out of our difficulties.

It is little wonder then that our society's response to the current sex-disease crisis has been primarily a technological one, rather than one that challenges sexual behaviour within a clear moral framework.[2]

While values such as commitment and fidelity within a monogamous relationship almost completely eliminate the risk of sexually transmitted disease providing there is no prior infection, the new 'value' being given the hard sell today is 'are you wearing a condom?' Increasingly sex education is seen as instruction, not in the art of developing fulfilling, committed relationships, but in the art of donning a condom. The arrival of AIDS has, without doubt, been a powerful driving force in the promotion of this new approach to sexual behaviour. The protection offered by the condom has now come to symbolise the hopes of all those who want disease-free sexual freedom or 'safe sex'. This is truly the 'Age of the condom'.

THE LIMITS OF TECHNOLOGY

But how reliable is this sexual technology? Remember we are dealing with potentially lethal diseases, and within the terms of the 'safe sex' philosophy it is the condom alone that is being asked to take the risk out of sexual intercourse.

First, what positive things can be said about the condom? Based on its physical properties alone the intact latex condom should provide an effective barrier against all known sexually transmitted agents including the AIDS virus, HIV.[3] Scanning electron microscope studies of samples taken from condom latex have shown that the wall structure is extremely fine and thus normally impermeable to even the smallest of the sexually transmitted disease (STD) agents, the hepatitus B virus.[4]

The condom is, however, a mass-produced item, and occasional manufacturing irregularities and defects will inevitably occur. As a safe-guard against sloppy manufacturing techniques, a sample of reputable brands is taken from the production line and then tested for quality against a known and agreed standard. The current British, American and international standards all specify that no more than 4 in 1000 condoms should have holes or tears at manufacture. These standards also reassuringly, it would seem, specify minimum values of wall thickness, rupture strength and stretch at rupture.[5] A 1991 Australian study published in the medical journal *Contraception*,[6] however, compared the tear strengths of used ruptured and unruptured condoms that had been returned. The condoms that had broken in 'service' were found to show similar strength properties to those that had not. The study concluded that the condom strength requirements specified in the manufacturing standards are not sufficient to insure a strong and therefore safe product. Of course a high strength condom could be designed so as never to rupture in service but it would hardly be acceptable to users because of the problem of discomfort.

It is generally accepted that the failure rate of condoms to prevent pregnancy is about 10 per cent per year.[7] Whereas pregnancy can only occur around ovulation, transmission of STDs can occur during intercourse at any time. Thus it is probably very conservative to assume even a figure as low as 10 per cent for the likely failure rate of condoms to prevent the passing of an STD.

WHAT IS THE BEST ADVICE?

In a special report in the American Medical Association Journal on preventing the heterosexual spread of AIDS, subtitled 'Are we giving our patients the best advice?'[8], important questions are raised concerning the advice given in the 'Safe Sex' program aimed at preventing spread of AIDS. The report conservatively assumes a risk factor for condom failure at 10 per cent per year. Some of its conclusions are:

1. Choosing a partner who is not in a high risk group provides a 5,000-fold degree of protection compared with a high risk group partner. By contrast condoms provide only a ten-fold degree of protection from the same high risk group partner.
2. Limiting the number of sexual partners *does not* necessarily reduce the risk of HIV infection. For example, having sexual intercourse 100 times with a partner who has a 1 per cent chance of being infected with HIV carries almost the same risk as having sexual intercourse one time each with 100 partners who each have a 1 per cent chance of being infected. This

arises because of the low infectivity of the HIV virus compared with most other STDs.

3. Using a condom with a high risk partner is far more dangerous than failing to use a condom with a partner who does not belong to a high risk group.

4. Encouraging the use of condoms in a high risk situation may even be dangerous as it can give a false sense of security.

The single most important advice conveyed in the above report is to choose one's partner very carefully. What is stressed is the need not only to ask potential partners about their present and past behaviour but also to get to know the person and his or her friends and family well enough to know whether or not to believe the answers. This, the report argues, rules out sex with prostitutes, casual sex, and much of what many people today would consider to be normal heterosexual behaviour.

In a Copenhagen study of condom rupture rates among both prostitutes and others practising normal heterosexual sex, an average rupture rate of 5 per cent was reported. This, combined with reported slippage rates of up to 15 per cent led the Danish researchers to conclude that 'truly safe sex with condoms is a dangerous illusion'.[9]

Ask any group of safe sex educators, 'Would you have sex with a person who had declared him or herself to have AIDS, using only a condom for protection?' and few would answer 'Yes'—for very obvious reasons. And yet this is precisely the game of sexual Russian roulette that is being sold today in the vigorous promotion of the safe sex programs.

These programs, specifically targeting young people and focussing largely on the mechanics of the sex act (i.e. love carefully— use a condom), are both morally deficient and technically flawed. There is great danger in removing the important moral dimension from sexual expression. Sexually active young people become too easily regarded as copulating machines requiring only contraceptive servicing. If we, as a society, genuinely desire to reduce the spread of STDs, a more responsible approach is required, one that recognises the all important ethical basis of human relationships. Casual sex, by its very definition, is characterised by a 'hit and run' exploitative mentality and largely excludes the possibility of truly knowing one's partner in a deeper sense, including a knowledge of disease. The ingredients of honesty, trust and commitment are necessary if there is to be a level of openness sufficient to provide any real certainty that the act of sexual intercourse will not carry a significant risk of STD.

ETHICAL CONSIDERATIONS

As our secular, pluralistic society struggles to come to terms with the STD crisis within a philosophical framework that is very largely dismissive of any real ethical reference points, Christians have a unique opportunity to present an alternative that is totally positive—in its affirmation of the marriage relationship, and positive in its assertion that the way ahead in human relationships need never be through the potentially lethal STD 'minefield'.

Jack Dominian, psychiatrist and Director of the UK Marriage Research Institute, offers some very constructive suggestions as to how Christians should address the human relational issues now brought into focus by the STD/AIDS crisis.[10] Dominian believes the way to tackle the problem is to ask what sex is for. He rightly argues that at the very heart of our sexuality as humans is the power of attraction, attachment and bonding:

Sexual intercourse [is] a body language

conveying the richest meaning of love, personal affirmation, confirmation of sexual identity, reconciliation, thanksgiving, and hope that the couple will remain the most important people in each other's lives. This is the inner world of intercourse, activated by sexual pleasure and the orgasm.

Such a view is thoroughly positive and provides a very sound basis for defining what Dominian calls 'sexual integrity'. Conversely he argues that indiscriminate sexual intercourse with 'instant bonding' denies the true meaning of the act.

The widespread loss of sexual integrity in our modern culture has unleashed a frighteningly destructive force which, as I have tried to show in this brief chapter, will take more than latex condoms to overcome.

NOTES
1. W Cates, 'Epidemiology and control of sexually transmitted diseases' in YM Felman (ed.), *Sexually transmitted diseases* (Churchill Livingstone, 1986), pp.1–22.
2. N D Broom and C E F Rickett, 'The ethics of safe sex' in *The New Zealand Medical Journal 101* (1988), pp. 823–826.
3. C A M Rietmeijer et al., 'Condoms as physical and chemical barriers against

human immunodeficiency virus', *Journal of the American Medical Association 259* (1988), pp. 1851–1853.

4. G Y Minuk et al., 'Efficacy of commercial condoms in the prevention of hepatitis B virus infection', *Gastroenterology 93* (1987), pp. 710–714.

5. Standard specifications for latex condoms: British (BS 3704); American (ASTM D 3492); International (ISO 4074).

6. J Gerofi, G. Shelley and B Donovan, 'A study of the relationship between tensile testing of condoms and breakage in use', *Contraception 43* (1991), pp. 177–185.

7. N B Williams (ed.), *Contraceptive technology 1986–1987* (Irvington, 1986), p. 102.

8. N Hearst and S B Hulley, 'Preventing the spread of AIDS—are we giving our patients the best advice?' *Journal of the American Medical Association 259* (1988), pp. 2428–2432.

9. P C Gøtzshe and M Hørding, 'Condoms to prevent HIV transmission do not imply truly safe sex', *Scandinavian Journal of Infectious Diseases 20* (1988), pp. 233–234.

10. J Dominian, 'Sexual morality today', a series of four articles published in *The London Tablet*, January 9, 16, 23 and 30, 1988. See also J Dominian, *Sexual integrity* (Darton, Longman and Todd, 1988).

♦ CHAPTER 8 ♦

The Bible and sexually transmitted diseases

GRANT GILLETT

When Justice Michael Kirby addressed the Legal Research Foundation Seminar on the legal implications of AIDS, in Auckland, New Zealand, in 1989, he stressed the fact that the control of AIDS was a matter for behavioural change rather than legislation.[1] AIDS is perhaps the most dramatic context in which we need to consider the relationships between sexuality, health and disease. Justice Kirby, and the gay groups commenting on this problem, have consistently stressed the central role for caring and fidelity in human sexual relationships. Their emphasis is instructive for our present purposes because it echoes the biblical foundations for sexuality and the control of sexually transmitted diseases (STDs).

Consider the following case:

George attends the STD clinic for a test because he has a painful discharge from his penis. He recounts several episodes where he has had casual sex with women he has met and gives the details of his most recent encounter. The tests are taken and he is duly informed that he has gonorrhoea. He remarks that the woman he slept with must have been a dirty, lying bitch and that he is really angry at her for infecting him. When asked to advise his wife about his disease he refuses because he doesn't want her to know. He is told of the risks and says that she is a big girl and can sort out her own problems if and when they arise. He expresses no regret about his own deception and casual sexual encounters, apart from anger at the woman who infected him, and he denies that there is any need to change his behaviour.

George presents a not uncommon face among those who develop STDs. The men involved often have quite distorted attitudes toward women and unrealistic perceptions of the moral aspects of their own behaviour. The type of situation he is in with its pathological mix of deceit, selfish gratification, and neither consideration for nor sensitivity to others, is all too often the norm in contemporary STD clinic experience.

BIBLICAL MEASURES

The biblical measures for the management of sexually transmitted diseases are recorded in the Pentateuch, in particular in Leviticus 15. They are set against a background norm of monogamy or at least of relationships in which partners were faithful to one another and families could be established. It is well recognised that the prevalence of venereal diseases bears a close relationship to the extent to which members of a community have multiple sexual partners. The penetration of STDs into a community is therefore dependent on infidelity in marriage or multiple pre-marital sexual partners. Those who work in STD clinics regularly note that where there is a background of strong marital commitment, despite the infidelity that has led to an STD being introduced into the partnership, the problem is solved and the disease treated quite readily. This contrasts with those situations where promiscuity is prevalent and there is a lack of commitment between sexual partners. The common situation, reflected in the case of George, is one in which we do not have to look far to find a complete lack of concern for the other person, a lack of any adequate conception of human well-being.

Fidelity and chastity

These facts add weight to arguments in favour of the biblical emphasis on fidelity and on chastity before marriage. The biblical laws relating to these diseases make it clear that venereal discharges are a sign of uncleanness and that those concerned should be treated in such a way that they cannot contaminate others and transmit the uncleanness. The injunctions are expressed in the language of ritual purity and indicate both an awareness of the infidelity which leads to infection and a sound, if sketchy, basis in the understanding of natural laws. The former awareness is not explicitly stated and is similar to the proscriptions applied to menstruating women (I shall come to these presently).

Provision for health and well-being

The transmission of venereal infections is

by person to person contact through sexual activity. Thus the only way to prevent transmission is to prevent sexual contact by infected persons. The biblical language of purity and impurity is one way to give and express due weight to this method of prevention. In fact, given that at the time the Bible was written there was not the detailed knowledge of infectious diseases that we now have, the idea of a contagious impurity is remarkably accurate. My thesis is that the biblical provisions, resting as they do on the foundation provided by a norm of settled and faithful relationships between men and women, reflect a profound awareness of what makes for human health and well-being. This thesis embodies some vital lessons about biblical wisdom, human well-being and moral law. In the purposes of God, the things that make for physical health and for spiritual well-being in human relationships belong together.

MORALITY AND NATURAL LAWS

There is a longstanding view in both secular and religious moral theory that what is moral is in some way connected with that life-style which is in the best interests of any given human being. This view is, however, not universally accepted. Whereas it seems natural for a Christian to believe that what God commands is directly tied to what he knows is good for us on the basis of his creative design, many secular moralists see no need to relate morality to well-being. Some would even see individual advantage as running counter to the moral claims of a society. The view that people might gain advantages by acting immorally, where they can get away with it, was explored by the great Greek philosophers of the 4th century BC, Plato and Aristotle.

1. Plato

Plato argued that to be fulfilled in all aspects of his being a man needs to take his proper place in the polis (the city-state) and to order his life on the model of the well-governed polis.[2] On both counts, Plato paid high regard to the role of reason and moral virtue. He saw the well-governed polis as having philosopher-kings as rulers, men pre-eminent in virtue and wisdom. The polis and the individual, in Plato's view, should be ruled by these qualities. Thus the Platonic man needed to be virtuous and intelligent in order to flourish. This implied that certain duties and responsibilities are an intrinsic part of the good life for any human being. Plato would not consider a person without a virtuous character to be functioning as he ought—he would be impaired in his well-being. While Plato's language and philosophy was limited in being sexist, elitist, and specifically related to the Greek conception of the democratic city state, nevertheless he recognised the link between personal well-being and moral practice.

2. Aristotle

Aristotle also recognised this same link between acting morally or virtuously and experiencing well-being. His view was based on observations about what gives distinct qualities to human life and the type of living that represents excellence. He considered such excellence to be the basis of human well-being. He argued, in a much more down to earth way than Plato, that friendship and virtue in personal relationships were intrinsic to that way of life. In his view, the life of virtue had rewards that were vastly greater than the pleasures of brutish or self-indulgent lives. Thus nature itself commended the moral life to those who wanted to live well.

3. Christian moralists

It is no accident that the early Christian moralists settled on Aristotle's theory of natural law. They noted that the teaching of Paul in Romans implied that God's law and his qualities could be seen in what he had made.[3] This was deeply congenial to Aristotle's thesis that an examination of the nature of human beings reveals that virtue and well-being are linked. Thus the adoption of Aristotelianism was almost irresistible.

We can therefore state a Christian natural law theory as follows: A Christian believes that human beings are created by God to function as co-creative and redemptive participants in the created order. We take our place in this arrangement according to God's grace revealed in Jesus Christ and through the faith given to us by the Holy Spirit. This relationship into which the believer comes is a fulfilment of inherent properties of human functioning that are able to be seen even where faith is not found. God has made the blueprint for good human living and then graciously revealed it through his word. But that blueprint carries within it firm guidelines as to how a human life can best be lived even when one has no inclination to live in faith toward God.

Christians therefore hold that there is a link between living well and living according to the law of God. In this claim they converge with one stream of secular moral theory that looks to the nature of humankind as a guide to what is good and right. Of course, for a Christian, goodness and rightness do not derive from human nature nor need support from secular philosophy; rather, they rest on the character of God, who created us and our world. This is a claim that goes beyond that made by a secular Aristotelian, but it follows from his view if one also holds the belief that nature runs according to the laws and grace of God.

I believe that Christians have a particularly strong case for this claim in the area of sexual love.

NATURAL LAW AND STDs

Laws of nature govern bacterial and viral life forms, their multiplication, their infectivity in human tissues, and the role of sexual intercourse in determining the patterns of spread of contagious diseases caused by them. These laws mean that there is a relationship between promiscuity and the incidence of STDs. To change this relationship would require the revision of an indeterminable number of eco-biological factors that regulate everyday human affairs. And even if, by this wholesale manipulation of nature, one were able to eliminate the possibility of STDs, one would still not modify the many other aspects of human sexuality that demonstrate the wisdom of the biblical pattern.[4] Thus, there are natural reasons, which include the facts about STDs, why fidelity and monogamy are to be preferred if one is to live a healthy life in the area of sexual relationships.

We ought to be quite clear about this claim. This is not the view that God created STDs to punish sinners for wayward sexual activity. Nor is it the view that sex is inherently unclean and nasty. It is a plain statement of the fact that sexual activity in this world carries certain natural consequences and that the biblical pattern reveals a certain wisdom about the avoidance and control of these consequences. The biblical commands to practise monogamy and fidelity, taken together with the procedures given in Leviticus for preventing the spread of an STD once detected, make good medical sense. They support the view that biblical morality is tied to human well-being. This indeed is what we would expect if such wisdom were a close reflection of the wisdom given by the Creator of the natural world. It does not, however, prove that all the commands in Leviticus and the particular imagery with which they are surrounded (taken literally) are valid for all time.

INTERPRETING BIBLICAL LAW

Whenever the main guidance for

Christian ethics comes from the Old Testament, we have to confront problems of legalism due to over-literal interpretations, in particular the misunderstanding of symbolism. Christ came to fulfil the law, and, in his dealing with the adulterous woman (as recorded in John 8:1-11), he showed that it might be applied with full spiritual force but without its punitive legal consequences.

The spiritual stress of Leviticus would seem to be on the concept of purity. In line with a dominant emphasis in Leviticus this purity stems ultimately from a due regard for the holiness of God; in human relationships this regard is to be expressed in love and fidelity, which the Bible as a whole so consistently emphasise. Purity of mind and purity of practice link the joy of sex to the context of a committed and caring relationship in which two people delight in each other through every aspect of their lives. This kind of relationship is the proper biblical setting for sexual intercourse and, for the reasons given above, it is essential to any remotely feasible program to eliminate STDs.

We must think carefully about how we should read the idea of impurity in Leviticus 15, where it is linked both to discharges arising from venereal infection and to normal menstrual discharges. This has certainly been interpreted in an oppressive way to reinforce stereotypes about uncleanness in women. The stigma attached to such ritual impurity is evident in the story of Jesus and the woman he healed from a discharge of blood (Luke 8:43-48). Indeed the problem of symbolism leading to oppressive social practices is not unique to the Bible. It seems to arise repeatedly as an expression of the insecurity felt by dominant male cultural groups in considering the roles and functions of women. This insecurity has often led to distortion in relationships between men and women. It tends to find symbolic expression in just the areas where the two differ and ought to complement one another. The symbols include fertility rituals, the sacrifice of young women, ritual prostitution, and numerous other institutions that portray women as mysterious, as 'man-traps' or as somehow infused with spiritual danger.

There is no suggestion of these darker distortions in the biblical texts, but it is natural that the facts to do with infection and transmission of contagious diseases, which I have already discussed, should find expression in this kind of language. The fact that such language has an evident cultural context does nothing to diminish the truths that it conveys; it is as understandable as other more superficial colloquialisms and idiomatic usage.

I have suggested that these ritual expressions in Leviticus can be interpreted in a positive way, as describing a practice that was well-grounded in natural law and was designed to minimise the spread of serious sexually transmitted disease including pelvic inflammatory disease (an infection in the uterus and fallopian tubes). The uterine lining is particularly susceptible to infection at certain times and around menstruation is one of those times. Thus it is natural for the injunctions against the spread of venereal disease to be linked to sexual practices at the time of menstruation. Again, we find that the biblical command is not arbitrary and has a plausible connection with facts of nature.

It remains unclear whether the practices outlined in Leviticus arise from empirical human observation or revelatory divine guidance. But we do not really need to decide between these options. Consider our attitude to medical science: we accept it as a gift from God and acknowledge that there are many ways in which the gift of knowledge is given. Medical knowledge may develop through the painstaking attention to nature that is evident in bio-medical research—or through a moment of inspiration that seems so fortuitous as to be God-given. A Christian will believe, in faith, that either way the knowledge is a gift of the Creator that we ought not to spurn and for which we can be thankful. In the same way we do not need to defend a thesis about God uttering, in ancient Hebrew, a series of instructions about STDs. The knowledge may have come much more gradually, yet still reflect providence and the Creator's law.

LAWS OF LOVE AND LAW OF NATURE

My underlying thesis has been that Old Testament law is eminently sensible in the way it deals with STDs. It is practicable in the light of contemporary knowledge, and, moreover, its stress on fidelity and non-promiscuity safeguard a kind of human well-being infinitely to be preferred to life in the kind of society in which STDs are rife. I have suggested that this reflects the fact that the Bible is not offering a series of commands about sexuality that seek to repress and restrict human living. Instead we ought to take careful note of those things the Bible seeks to emphasise. The more we find out about topics such as STDs, the more it becomes clear that the biblical wisdom encapsulates important perspectives on the way human beings ought to live and relate to one another.

I have conceded that the biblical language may resort to imagery that is no longer entirely appropriate to contemporary dialogue and can be interpreted to embody certain attitudes that we no longer find morally acceptable. This is entirely consistent with the view that biblical wisdom is a record of the dealings of a loving God as recorded by fallible human authors (writing, I believe, under an inspiration sufficient to protect them from error).[5]

In the area of STDs the medical community has learned a few hard lessons, particularly from cases like that of George. What are those lessons?

1. We have learned that the incidence and seriousness of sexually transmitted disease in a society reflect the sexual behaviour of that society.

2. We have realised that attitudes rather than antibiotics or other wonder drugs are the central issue in attempts to control STDs.

3. We have noticed that attitudes of fidelity, trust and commitment are central in the prevention and the resolution of the states of physical and mental ill-health that arise from such diseases.

4. We have therefore come to adopt practices in dealing with STDs which, while not having an intentionally moral thrust, are nevertheless convergent with biblical wisdom.

NOTES

1. M Kirby, 'Legal implications of AIDS' in *Legal Implications of AIDS*, ed R Paterson (Legal Research Foundation, Auckland, 1989).
2. Plato's *Republic* argues this at length in its attempt to commend a life of justice and virtue.
3. Romans 1, especially verses 18–21.
4. These aspects of sexuality are discussed elsewhere in this volume.
5. Error, in this context, does not preclude the fact that, if taken literally, certain passages of the Bible may be misapplied in ways that go beyond inspiration and authority. This does not impugn the scriptural record; it merely urges us to be cautious in our use and intepretation of it.

◆ CHAPTER 9 ◆

Homosexuality

COLIN BECROFT AND
IAN HOOKER

We approach the question of homosexuality as Christians who thank God for his gift of life and salvation. That gift of life includes our sexuality. We share the widespread concern as to what our attitude should be towards those who are called homosexual and we acknowledge with sorrow that in the course of history both society and the church have treated homosexuals with suspicion and cruelty. In recent years the attitudes of society have greatly changed to the point where homosexual practice is sometimes presented, even in the church, as an acceptable alternative to heterosexual behaviour.

As we discuss homosexuality we acknowledge our fallibility. We respect the validity of scientific research; we honour the supremacy of Scripture in all debate concerning human conduct and we wish to 'speak the truth' as we understand it 'in love'.

TERMS AND PRACTICES

It may be helpful at the outset to be clear about terms and practices. Homosexuality is the term for same sex love, that is the erotic attraction of a man for a man, or a woman for a woman. Male homosexuals often prefer to be called 'gay', and women 'lesbians'. We use the term 'homosexual' to refer to either. (The prefix 'homo-' in the word homosexual does not mean 'man' as in 'homo sapiens' but 'same' as in 'homogeneous'.) Heterosexual is the term used for the person attracted to someone of the opposite sex. 'Bisexuals' regularly experience both heterosexual and homosexual attraction.[1] 'Transvestites' dress as for the opposite sex and experience detachment from their own sex. 'Transsexuals' feel as if they are the opposite sex; thus a male transsexual feels as if he is a woman trapped in a man's body.

It is important to be clear about what constitutes homosexual activity. A close homosexual relationship usually involves holding hands, cuddling and kissing. In the case of male homosexuality this frequently leads to mutual masturbation and oral sex. There may also be sexual intercourse by penetration of the anus, which creates serious danger of physical damage and of infection and spread of disease. Unlike the vagina, the rectum is not reinforced to provide for penetration. In the case of females, fondling may lead to mutual masturbation, oral sex, or the use of artificial objects for penetration. Men frequently have numerous casual contacts; women tend more often to enter into nurturing relationships.

The facts of anatomy speak for themselves: male and female bodies are similar but different. Our reproductive organs correspond and are clearly intended to be complementary.

A SCRIPTURAL UNDERSTANDING

The foundational statements of Genesis 1:27-28 and 2:24 have been considered in chapter 2 of this book. They show that when God created humankind in his own image, he did so by creating them male and female, that is as complementary beings. These passages go on to state that God bade them join together and be fruitful. Sexuality therefore is the 'God-given impulse that draws a man and a woman together'[2], and marriage involves a male and a female who are permanently and publicly committed to each other and who jointly consummate their union.

1. The teaching of Jesus

In continuity with this Genesis theme, Matthew 19:4 contains a central statement of the teaching of Jesus with regard to sexual activity. Here our Lord reaffirms the state of heterosexual marriage (he affirms no other) in terms of the foundational words: 'Have you not read that the one who made them the beginning "made them male and female" . . .'? He thus appeals to 'God's purpose of unity in marriage'.[3]

Jesus explains that some people will not marry (verse 12). Either they are born unable to marry or they become unable to marry as a result of the actions of others. Some, who voluntarily renounce the possibility 'for the sake of the kingdom', may accept a life of chastity in order to serve God and humanity unencumbered. They may be called to be pioneer missionaries under rugged conditions that preclude normal married life, or they may willingly undertake some other responsibility such as the care of elderly parents.

In Matthew 19 therefore we are confronted with an ideal. Whatever our personal biological heritage and sexual orientation, we have two choices as Christians: to live our lives either in heterosexual marriage or in sexual abstinence. Down the centuries thousands upon thousands of our fellow Christians, women and men, have committed their lives to God in this way. While at various times, including our own day, the ideal has been tarnished by all manner of deviations and extremes, this word of our Lord continues to stand as a lighthouse. Chastity is the issue for all and it applies both to the homosexual and to the heterosexual. Like many other challenges posed by scripture, it calls for willingness to face reality and for reliance on the power of the Holy Spirit if it is to be lived out.

2. The teaching of Paul

As indicated earlier in this book, the apostle Paul looks to this same Genesis passage as the basis for his teaching on the mutual love and respect of the husband and wife as the foundation of human families (Ephesians 5:31). He is appealing to the 'fundamental order of creation'.[4] By contrast, when he refers to women and men who, instead of natural intercourse, indulge in 'degrading [same sex] passions' (Romans 1:26-27), he sees this as the inevitable result of serving the creature rather than the Creator, resulting in 'a debased mind and . . . things that should not be done' (1:28). Not only does Paul speak about the wrong of those who engage in homosexual activities and other actions he has listed, but he speaks of the guilt of those who 'applaud others who prac- tise them' (Romans 1: 32).

When Paul catalogues certain wrong kinds of behaviour for the Corinthian church (1 Corinthians 6:9-11), he includes homosexual activity. It is questionable to suggest, as some do, that here (and also in Romans 1) we have merely an early Church list of vices that are not so important for us. If in fact Paul was quoting, we may be sure he did not do so lightly or carelessly.

Helmut Thielicke, in the course of a very compassionate treatment, writes:

There can be no doubt that Paul regards homosexuality as a sin and a perversion of the order of human existence willed by God. . . The homosexual must therefore be willing to be treated or healed so far as this is possible; he must, as it were, be willing to be brought back into the 'order'.[5]

3. Scriptural attitudes

Scripture gives no hint that homosexual relationships should be viewed as parallel to marriage. We may conclude that, whatever our heredity or the tendencies we discover within ourselves, we Christians have the task of directing our lives responsibly in accordance with the foundational statement of Genesis as developed in the New Testament.

It is worthy of note, however, that nowhere in Scripture is there condemnation of homosexual orientation as such. In Old Testament society it was homosexual activity that was forbidden (Leviticus 18:22, 20:13).

We who live by the grace of God are certainly not to be judgmental. The New Testament portrays Jesus dealing more gently with those who committed sins of the flesh than those who committed sins of the spirit. When a woman taken in adultery was being condemned by others, Jesus said, 'Neither do I condemn you. Go your way; and from now on do not sin again' (John 8:11). He made a firm moral judgment without being judgmental. We do well to act in the same spirit.

THE CURRENT UNDERSTANDING

For many generations attitudes to homosexuals have been based on ignorance and prejudice. The New Testament ideals and patterns for Christian people were translated into secular law and given Old Testament punitive sanctions. The heterosexual majority, often suffering from what is now termed homophobia and unaware of their own repressed fears and guilt, forced homosexuals underground. Even during the past hundred years disclosure and public scandal have sometimes been followed by prosecution and prison.

Shortly after World War II, the British government appointed a Commission to review the body of long-standing and in many respects seriously outdated law governing sexual behaviour. As a result of the ensuing Wolfenden Report, homosexual activity in private between consenting adults ceased to be a criminal offence in Great Britain. Similar steps were taken in other countries. Since then there has been a tremendous upsurge of gay and lesbian activism and, simultaneously, widespread relaxation in the attitudes of society. Some are now calling for a new morality that will accept mutually committed homosexual relationships alongside heterosexual marriage. Nevertheless, homophobia is still widespread.

ATTITUDES IN THE COUNSELLING PROFESSION

The counselling professions have tended to follow the lead of the American Psychiatric Association, which has de-emphasised the classification of homosexuality in the Diagnostic and Statistical Manual of Mental Disorders. However the current edition, known as DSM-III-R, does include 'persistent and marked distress about one's sexual orientation' within its category of psychosexual disorders. The international statistical classification has not made this change. There is a body of professional opinion that sees the occurrence of homosexuality in a family as an indication that treatment, perhaps for the whole family, may be desirable.

In the reasonably mature family, both parents model for their same-sex children the art of relating to the opposite sex. They also affirm the respective masculinity and femininity of their opposite-sex children. Some children suffer when a parent is absent or finds it emotionally difficult to fulfil these functions. A wide variety of circumstances such as illness, death or external influences may have their effect in otherwise problem free families. Some parents are unduly strict, insensitive, or emotionally distant.

Most couples bring unfinished and unrecognised 'baggage' from their original families to their marriages and to their resultant families. There is an increasing number of families in which marital problems and abuse adversely affect children, perhaps prenatally, and certainly during early developmental years. It seems probable that where homosexual orientation occurs the seeds were planted at a very early stage.

RECENT RESEARCH

A promising model of understanding is that provided by Dr Elizabeth Moberly's research. She contends that the homosexual, as a child, has suffered some deficit in the same-sex parental attachment that normally encourages a male to become masculine, and a female feminine. This may be due to failure in parental behaviour, but is not necessarily so. Typical examples are early separation, emotional unavailability, or harsh behaviour of the same-sex parent. The resulting detachment—'you have hurt me by not loving me'—becomes dis-identification—'You have hurt me, I don't want to be like you.'

Dr Moberly goes on to point out that from this detachment comes a corresponding drive for same-sex love. This is an appropriate reparative endeavour to resolve and heal the damage. 'The homosexual condition does not involve abnormal needs, but normal needs that have, abnormally, been left unmet in the ordinary process of growth'.[6] 'The male homosexual is like a young boy still looking for father's love. The lesbian is like a young girl still looking for mother's love'.[7] Meeting these needs erotically is inappropriate: a confusion of the legitimate needs of a child—to be affirmed and nurtured—with the physically mature sexual needs of adulthood. The result is that these needs will not be adequately met. Can they be met legitimately? Dr Moberly says they can, and we refer to this below.

CAUSES AND CHOICES

Some homosexual individuals state that their orientation and life style is a matter of their own personal choice. Nowadays, however, the gay movement actively promotes the idea that homosexuality is given, perhaps inherited, and cannot be changed. It is remarkable that while the Human Potential movement has emphasised the freedom of human beings to make individual choices and to develop their distinctive individual life styles, those in church and society who plead for acceptance of homosexual behaviour tend to assert vigorously that homosexuality is not a choice but is predetermined at birth. Wide publicity has been given recently to such claims based on research on brain structures, and on studies of twins. Other researchers, however, offer alternative interpretations of the data, and much more work remains to be done. The debate over genetic, hormonal and environmental causes of human conditions is likely to continue indefinitely.

RESPONSIBILITY FOR ACTIONS

It appears unlikely that any one theory can sufficiently explain such a complex issue, or the great diversity of distinctly different individuals and families who are involved. There may be factors that produce a tendency, but none will exempt the individual from the responsibility of choice. For example, antisocial behaviour is thought to be influenced both by heredity and by experience in the original family. It does not follow that violent offenders are not accountable. Awareness of an orientation, or the experience of a strong desire, does not confer the right to act upon it; the commandment against adultery is evidence for that.

Christian people in particular have to

decide whether to yield to the prevailing spirit of the age or to direct their actions with loyalty to the Lord in the light of Holy Scripture. Irrespective of what is discovered, a fundamental question remains for all of us to answer—'Whether my particular condition is inherited or acquired, and whatever it may be, what shall I do with it and what is my response to temptation?'

THE POSSIBILITY OF CHANGE

The Apostle Paul appears to have had no doubt about the possibility of change. After including certain types of practising homosexuals among the 'wrongdoers (who) will not inherit the kingdom of God', he makes the decisive statement 'This is what some of you used to be.' (1 Corinthians 6:11). If such change occurred in the church of Corinth, why should it not occur in the church today? Many gay and lesbian activists say they have reached the point of no return and encourage others to feel the same. We ask them to think again. The stories of Michael, Julie and George at the end of this chapter, along with numerous others, testify to what is possible. It is cruel to deny the possibility of change to oneself or to others who struggle with these issues.

There have been a number of reviews of

results obtained in various projects where homosexuals have undertaken psychotherapy with a view to possible change. Percentages of those who reported change have varied, and in some cases the depth or length of change is not clear. Two researchers[8] have reported in fascinating depth on a group of eleven formerly active homosexuals who have become associated with a church. After four years of counselling and support, eight had become 'emotionally detached from homosexual identity in both behaviour and intrapsychic (i.e. internal) process, three were functionally heterosexual with some evidence of neurotic conflict.' Six were married, eight were 'helping their peers as ex-homosexuals' and reported 'no homosexual arousal.' In each case Christian awakening, spiritual development and positive acceptance by their church group had gone hand in hand with counselling. It appeared that the religious and spiritual factor was very significant. The authors conclude that 'when homosexuality is defined as an unchangeable and fixed condition that must be accepted, the potential for change seems slim; when defined as a changeable condition, it appears that change [is] possible.'

While few churches have benefited from similar professional research, more and more churches around the world, and organisations such as Exodus, report a continuing flow of troubled homosexuals who learn to accept a life style of abstinence or go on to discover heterosexual orientation and satisfying marriage. This usually comes about following the combination of spiritual renewal and counselling with friendship and support. Some fall, but rise again; it is seldom an easy pathway.

A PATHWAY FOR CHANGE

Dr Moberly has mapped out a pathway for change. 'Substitute relationships for parental care are in God's redemptive plan, just as parental relationships are in his creative plan'.[9] What is needed is Gender-Affirmative Therapy with a same-sex therapist, encouraging same-sex identity, resolving same-sex hurts from the past, while abstaining from premature pressure towards relationships with the opposite sex. Preferably this will be backed up by loving, lasting, same-sex, non sexual relationships, especially in the church. She concludes,

Love, both in prayer and in relationships is the basic therapy. . . the great need, the only true solution. If we are willing to seek and mediate the healing and

redeeming love of Christ, then healing for
the homosexual will become a great and
glorious reality.[10]

How is it that work such as this has so
far received so little attention? Certainly the
gay movement has worked aggressively to
sell its point of view. But there is a deeper
problem. We human beings, whatever our
beliefs and values, frequently have a strong
unconscious set against digging deeply into
the self in ways that might risk shaking loose
our long held misconceptions. For many of
us, the possibility of change requires that we
pray with the same desperate faith as Augustine, 'I beseech you God to show my full self
to myself'.[11] His words are in line with the
Psalmist's 'Clear me from hidden faults.'
'You desire truth in the inward being. . .
teach me wisdom in my secret heart' (Psalms
19:12 and 51:6).

RESOURCES TO HELP

'Heterosexuality is a by-product of building a secure same-sex identity'.[12] Resources
are available through Exodus Ministries and
similar groups and individuals who offer
therapy and support based on

(a) discovering the source of emotional
arrest in the past;

(b) learning to face attitudes of anger, unforgivingness, bitterness towards those who hurt us;

(c) reinforcing our personhood in wholesome same-sex friendships;

(d) learning to identify and break the triggering patterns of addictive sexual behaviour by replacing [them with new] patterns;

(e) identifying confusion and establishing true gender identity.

Exodus believes that this can be effective 'to the degree that the client allows the Holy Spirit freedom to work in his or her life and is prepared to co-operate positively.'

We owe it to gays and lesbians to offer help in tracing the early origins of their condition, with a view to discovering their heterosexual potential. Sadly, many activists are not prepared to admit that they might benefit from looking at the possibility of change.

We make this practical proposal for any person who feels that he or she is homosexually or bisexually oriented: Undertake psychotherapy with the agreed purpose of discovering if there were factors in your family of origin that could possibly have predisposed you in that direction. At the same time find a mature spiritual mentor who will encourage and pray with you in your quest, and stand alongside you in your struggle. We encourage the reader to believe in the possibility of change.

THE ROLE OF THE CHURCH

For ministry in the Church to be helpful, we must learn to see and value people as our Lord does and win the right to help them deal with their problems. We all have problems we struggle with. If there is to be an environment of love, acceptance and understanding in which people feel able to be open about their inner selves, we will need to remember that 'by grace [we] have been saved through faith . . . not the result of works' (Ephesians 2: 8-9). So in the spirit of the New Testament we will not condemn homosexuals, whether gay or lesbian. In fact we suggest that from now on wherever possible we do not use those terms, even when people label themselves that way, lest we stamp the condition to the person. It is worth noting that in a parallel situation we are advised against referring to someone as 'an alcoholic'; the correct designation is 'has an alcohol problem' or is 'alcohol dependent'.

It goes without saying that negative, destructive language and jokes concerning the homosexual condition are totally unacceptable. We should also bear in mind that there are within our churches quiet, anonymous people who struggle with homosexuality, who may never have been in the so-called 'gay scene' or experienced a homosexual relationship, but who live in constant fear of being discovered and rejected. In some churches, if they pluck up courage to speak to someone about their concerns, they risk being shunned, even by ministers (usually out of ignorance and fear).

FACILITATING FRIENDSHIPS

The facilitation of friendships is of prime importance. The Bible contains instances of warm same-sex relationships like those between Ruth and Naomi, David and Jonathan, Jesus with Peter and James and John, Paul and Timothy. Such relationships are healthy where there is mutual respect, honesty, and equality. They are unhealthy when there is dominance or servile dependency. Developing a number of friendships reduces the likelihood of a dependent relationship on one person.

'God has poured out his love into our hearts by the Holy Spirit, whom he has given us' (Romans 5:5 NIV). Here is our inexhaustible source of true love. The person who suffers from childhood deficits has great need of that unconditional acceptance. Someone whose early relationship with father or mother was damaged may need to experience trust over a long period in order to build a right concept of God as a loving, supportive father. As our love needs are met in Christ and through his body the church, we can begin to meet the love needs of others. 'Beloved, let us love one another, for love is from God' (1 John 4:7).

We do not discount possession by a spirit of evil. The prayer 'deliver us from evil' has not lost its power over lust, anger, and despair. But the treatment for the basic condition of homosexuality is a combination of loving support and counselling. The loving exercise of discipline may be required, especially when persons in leadership or teaching positions persist in sexual sin, homosexual or heterosexual[13].

In counselling, a listening ear will encourage people to begin looking at themselves and working through their problems. Sympathetic professional help will be valuable in areas where people are stuck. Outside support may be helpful, especially if available from people who have worked through these issues themselves.

THREE JOURNEYS

We conclude by relating the personal journeys of three people. We are grateful for their willingness to share their stories with others. Names and some details have been changed to ensure anonymity.

1. Michael

Michael came near the end of a big family of boys. His memories are of a strong, authoritarian sports loving father, and a distant mother who left the family before he had reached his teens. The domestic role vacuum after his mother's departure was eventually filled by Michael himself. He was attempting to gain his father's approval and praise, but that seemed to be reserved for the rest of his sports loving brothers rather than for him.

Michael's school days were difficult. His Maori culture had been rejected by his own Maori father. In his emotional uncertainty Michael felt he did not fit in anywhere. More tragedy entered his life at fifteen when he was sexually molested by a close family friend. This continued for the next nine months, and so great was the sense of guilt and shame that he never told anyone. He was in conflict, trapped in homosexual fantasies and compulsive masturbation, becoming more and more aware of growing homosexual feelings. Yet there was a positive event that gave him hope, for he committed himself to Christ at a Billy Graham rally.

Michael left home at twenty-three. A few years later a young man moved into his flat. As Michael was comforting this young man at a time of great grief over the death of both parents, a deep emotional and physical homosexual relationship developed that lasted for eighteen months. This was broken when both young men finally decided that their relationship was contrary to God's will and both confessed to the elders of their church. The elders were understanding and supportive, and encouraged them to undertake counselling.

Over the following twelve months, Michael worked intensively through false beliefs about himself that had dominated his behaviour and through the deep anger he felt towards his father. He needed to deal with the unforgiving bitterness that governed his life. The process of change began and has continued for several years. Today he has left his old lifestyle behind and is developing a healthy relationship with a young woman in his church.

2. Julie

Julie was aged twenty-four when she sought help. The oldest of her family, she had been raised in a Christian home. Her father was quiet and somewhat emotionally distant; her mother took the strong disciplinary role. Love shown to the children by the parents seemed to be conditional on meeting certain standards of performance.

As a youngster Julie was unhappy and had a great sense of shame, guilt, and self blame because of her inability to meet those standards. (Today she does not blame her parents, for she realises they were only doing their best, with the understanding they had, to raise her as a morally upright person.) Her early teenage experiences with boys were unhappy, which led to more self blaming and doubt.

During nursing training she experienced her first strong emotional attachment to a fellow nurse, but was put down badly when the other woman realised what was happening. For some years she did not allow her feelings for women to come to the surface again. Then, while living in a commune overseas, she became attracted to one of the other women, and on this occasion the feelings were reciprocated. For the next two years she was involved in an intense emotional and physical relationship.

All this time her guilt was increasing as she became more aware that what she was doing was incompatible with her faith in Christ. She broke off the relationship, and entered a Bible college with the hope of getting the help she needed. The academic thrust of college did not help her deal with her problems; in fact her feelings of shame and isolation increased. She developed emotional attachments for two of her women fellow students, but did not reveal them.

It was after graduation that Julie sought help and began a long slow process of dealing with the hurts and shame of the past, as the love of God was brought to bear on the wounds of childhood and on the destructive negative thinking that pervaded her life. In the years that followed, through the help of many fine Christian friends, she learned how to have healthy relationships with both men and women.

Today, nearly ten years later, Julie is happily married to a minister, is the mother of a small child and is very content with her life. She was asked how much she had changed in terms of the Kinsey Scale. This controversial scale runs from 0 (exclusively heterosexual, attracted only to the opposite sex)[14] to 7 (an exclusive homosexual bias, attracted only to the same sex.) She replied that she felt she had moved from a '6' to a '2'.

3. George

George was shattered when he was diagnosed as HIV positive. Now, years later, he hopes that ongoing research may yet allow him to die of old age. He had first become aware that he was 'different' on reaching puberty, when he lost most of his friends. They were becoming interested in girls while he was being 'turned on' by his male heroes.

After leaving secondary school, George was fondled sexually by a self-styled health expert. In his need to be loved, he began to enjoy cuddling with a boy friend. Although he had always attended church, in his own words, 'My heart had not yet been touched by Jesus'. A church-related youth group got through to him and he 'became a real Christian'. Not being comfortable about his sexual orientation, he began consulting respected leaders. Most were baffled. Two diagnosed demon possession and undertook exorcism, which he found irrelevant and also humiliating when his confidence was abused. A noted counsellor told him to accept his condition as God-given. (Today George is a widely travelled and mature

Christian. When he looks back on that advice he thinks of it as 'the worst thing that ever happened to me'.)

George soon discovered that when he and another homosexual met casually on the street, they were likely to experience instant mutual recognition in each other's eyes. He notes that the homosexual culture lacks the norms that protect people in the 'straight' world. And so from time to time he found himself plunging into the gay scene, sometimes uninhibitedly. He got to know the full range of the gay lifestyle. Ultimately, he came to realise that 'gay activity shattered my Christian life; my walk with my Lord suffered'. Repentance and forgiveness became very real to him.

While George has been deeply involved in prominent churches of his denomination in several places, only one has given him the opportunity to identify his orientation and to enjoy fellowship with a group of homosexuals who were making an honest attempt to encourage one another in controlling their sexuality appropriately. This group also made a concerted effort to reach out to the gay bars with the love of Christ.

Today, coping with gayness is George's biggest challenge. He has been free of homosexual activity for several years. He finds the gay churches unacceptable. He feels they tend to serve a double purpose. He is tremendously grateful for several Christian friends and a group who share his background with whom he can be honest and pray. His realistic appraisal is that the more actively people have experienced the gay scene, the less likely it is that they will change their orientation. He observes that very few gays continue their relationships long-term; those who do, while continuing their commitments as friends, tend to seek sexual expression elsewhere.

HOPE FOR THE FUTURE

The issue of homosexuality is deep and complex, and there are no simple answers. Results may take years; some never see results at all. But the stories of Michael, Julie and George are matched by numerous others around the world. We can pray that 'the grace of the Lord Jesus Christ, and the love of God, and the fellowship of the Holy Spirit . . . ' (2 Corinthians 13:14) will be their guide and support, and ours.

Practical guidelines for individual helpers and church based ministries

(With acknowledgments to Exodus and others.)

1. Provide a context of loving care from

friends, without sex. Relate to a person, not to a classification. Don't be afraid to touch, hug and say 'I love you'. Offer Christ, not an ethical code. Maintain a discreet, non-militant profile, with prayer.

2. Offer confidence, for many will be fearful. Be prepared for raw language from those who know only street talk.

3. Patience, and yet more patience is essential. Homosexual feelings are not likely to change overnight. Stick with your friend when the going is tough. Acknowledge readily when you don't have an answer.

4. This work may be emotionally draining. Keep in close touch with your minister or other approved facilitator.

5. Only lawyers and doctors should give legal or medical advice. Keep a list of trusted, competent individuals, drug and AA programs and other agencies.

6. A local church should count the cost with care if involved in setting up a counselling program.

   • Non-professional helpers should be screened and trained and should usually work in pairs (married couples, two women, two men).

   • All helpers should discuss their contacts regularly with a qualified supervisor. Provision should be made for continuing education.

- To avoid misunderstanding and false accusations, do not hold counselling sessions in private homes. Never give out home addresses or phone numbers.

- Observe confidentiality; never divulge information without the written consent of the counsellee.

- Reports of all sessions (including counselling by phone) and records of letters received and sent should be kept under lock and key.

Note: For addresses of parallel organisations in various countries and localities, refer to Exodus International, PO Box 2121, San Rafael, CA 94912, USA.

NOTES

1. The House of Bishops of the Church of England in their recent statement, *Issues in human sexuality* (Church House Publishing, 1991) comments 'it is clear that bisexual activity must always be wrong for this reason, if for no other, that it inevitably involves being unfaithful' (p. 42).

2. *New Oxford Annotated Bible*, NRSV, note on Genesis 2:24.
3. *New Oxford Annotated Bible*, note on Matthew 19:5.
4. Helmut Thielicke, *The ethics of sex* (Harper, 1964), p.282. Note also the above quoted statement by the House of Bishops, which goes on to say (p.40) that homosexuality and heterosexuality are not alternative forms of sexuality 'as complete within the terms of the created order' and are not 'congruous with the observed order of creation or with the insights of revelation.'
5. Helmut Thielicke, *op.cit.*, pp. 278, 283.
6. Elizabeth Moberly, *Homosexuality: a new Christian ethic* (James Clarke, 1983), p.28.
7. Elizabeth Moberly, personal communication, June 16 1992.
8. E M Pattison and M L Pattison, ' "Ex-gays": religiously mediated change in homosexuals' in *The American Journal of Psychiatry, December 1980*, pp.1553–1562.
9. Elizabeth Moberly, *op.cit.*, pp. 35–36.
10. *Ibid.*, p.52.
11. Augustine, *Confessions*, Book 10.
12. Elizabeth Moberly, personal communication, 16 June 1992.
13. The *Report of the House of Bishops* referred to above, a document that is very

compassionate towards homosexuals, comes to this conclusion (p.45) about practising homosexuals in the ordained ministry:

We have, therefore, to say that in our considered judgment the clergy cannot claim the liberty to enter into sexually active homophile relationships. Because of the distinctive nature of their calling, status and consecration, to allow such a claim on their part would be seen as placing that way of life in all respects on a par with heterosexual marriage as a reflection of God's purposes in creation. The Church cannot accept such a parity and remain faithful to the insights which God has given it through Scripture, tradition and reasoned reflection on experience.

14. See Judith A Reisman and Edward W Eichel, *Kinsey, sex and fraud*, edited by John H Court and J Gordon Muir (Lochinvar—Huntington House, 1990). These investigators and others have examined Kinsey's methods and uncovered disturbing violations of acceptable standards of research. These are sufficiently serious as to throw grave doubts

on many of his conclusions. The evidence they present includes selection of unrepresentative subjects, for example a higher percentage of prisoners and sexual offenders. This continued in spite of warnings and criticism, which Kinsey received from the late Dr Abraham Maslow who is noted for his research and writings on human personality and potential. The result was gross exaggeration in the percentage of persons thought to be homosexual. Kinsey gave the figure as ten per cent of the male population whereas his raw data support a figure of only one or two per cent. He also arranged the perpetration of numerous sex acts on children, which he represented as scientific research, with suggestions that adult/child sex can be beneficial to children.

RECOMMENDED READING

John Stott, *Issues facing Christians today* (Marshall, Morgan and Scott, 1984), ch.16.

Elizabeth R Moberly, *Homosexuality: A new Christian ethic* (James Clarke, 1983).

William Consiglio, *Homosexual no more* (Victor Books, 1991).

David Field, *The homosexual way* (Inter-Varsity Press, 1979).

◆ CHAPTER 10 ◆

Gender and homosexuality

HAROLD TURNER

CURRENT SHAPE OF THE QUESTION

Recently there has been intense discussion among Christians in the areas of gender and homosexuality, conducted in terms of 'sexuality', and focused especially on the two forms of hetero- and homo-sexuality. In relation to the latter there are at least three distinct issues and considerable progress has been made since the 1970s in dealing with two of these.

The first, decriminalisation of consenting homosexual behaviour, was long overdue. The Christian opposition to decriminalisation was based on the belief that such a procedure implies acceptance of homosexuality in general. In fact, decriminalisation was a first step in removing harsh, punitive attitudes in both Church and State.

The second step was the new pastoral attitude that sees homosexuals not so much judgmentally but rather as people to understand and relate to lovingly and responsibly. Official church statements and most people in pastoral ministry now express this attitude, even if many church members have not yet caught up.

The discussion now concentrates on a third issue: the acceptance of those living in a full homosexual partnership not only into church membership but also into the ordained ministry. Many of those who have campaigned for the above-mentioned first two changes see this as the logical conclusion to the process of change. They, perhaps rather wishfully, assume that the new pastoral attitudes imply the normalisation of homosexuality. Others, a majority, have seen these new attitudes as no more than a fully Christian approach to this as to any other aspect of human behaviour, and as having nothing to do with reclassifying homosexuality as 'right'. This unidentified difference of interpretation has bedevilled current discussion.

Language and limits for our discussion

Beyond the current divisions of opinion on these issues the one inescapable feature we all share is the fact of our sexuality, which is given to us in the form of our gender. We must all have parents of the two genders and we are all born either male or female. Some would play down the effect of 'nature', i.e. genetic origins and physical differences. They would emphasise the subsequent influence of 'nurture' in a particular culture in establishing our gender and our sexual orientation. Others argue for the reverse emphasis. There is probably no way of settling the balance of these two groups of factors, either for any individual or as a general rule. Since for the purposes of our exploration here this question does not first have to be settled, we need spend no more time on it.

Likewise we can avoid being embroiled in attempts to stereotype the two genders in terms of different masculine and feminine 'qualities', or to do the reverse, to eliminate differences and see humankind in unisex terms. The biological distinctions between men and women are permanent and pervasive. They can neither be eliminated nor sloughed off after they have served a reproductive purpose for some of us. We live our whole lives as men or women, apart from a tiny proportion of trans-sexuals and transvestites. The holistic emphasis in modern thought points to the interaction of body and mind.

Gender must not be identified with sexuality. The latter may find expression between the genders ('hetero-'), or within either gender ('homo-', and then as either 'gay' or 'lesbian'). The forms of gender expression vary from the implicit and unconscious factor in all relationships between men and women to the more overtly sexual forms. Sexuality as a drive, an activity or an experience is endlessly variable, comes and goes, waxes and wanes. But through all these variations the invariable fact of gender remains, and it is the wider term.

Again gender is presupposed by marriage but does not require marriage, much less parenthood, for its significance. Some men and women may by choice *become* related as husband and wife, but all men and women *are* related as male and female and here there is no choice between gender or no gender.

Trans-sexuals and sex-change operations only illustrate the point. The fact that Jesus was neither married nor a parent, but nevertheless possessed gender enabled him to be thoroughly human, and let us say at once no more human than if the incarnation had been in the form of a female.

Some ethical theory and basic theology

The arguments for the radical reclassification of homosexuality have been conducted in terms of sexuality tahter than Gender, from which sexuality can be distinguished but not separated, has tended to be ignored. Those who oppose any aspect of this comprehensive reclassification have often found themselves discussing the issue in the terms chosen by those who support the new attitudes, even while they felt uneasy in so doing. At the same time they have not found it easy to formulate their own understanding in a way that is convincing to themselves or to others. Although able to explain decriminalisation and support a more positive pastoral approach, they have been left with little more than an inarticulate 'gut reaction' against the public acceptance of homosexuals into the Christian ministry.

The fact that this reaction is inarticulate does not mean that it is erroneous. Michael

Polanyi, an influential scientist-philosopher dealing with the ways in which we know truth, has taught us that most of our knowledge of truth is in fact implicit or 'tacit knowledge'. We always 'know more than we can tell', much less actually 'prove'. Our knowledge about right and wrong, truth and error, always exceeds our capacity to articulate this knowledge. 'Gut knowledge' is therefore to be taken seriously, even though we should always work at making it more explicit and then critiquing it.

To articulate and examine our implicit knowledge in this area is to engage in moral philosophy or ethical theory, and in Christian theology. This essay aims to help us undertake some fairly simple but basic thinking, to 'do' some ethics and some theology. In acquiring these tools we will also be able to examine the presentation of the homosexual position by its convinced supporters.

MORAL ARGUMENTS USED IN THE DISCUSSION

The presentation of the homosexual position is couched in moral rather than theological language, and upon analysis it reveals at least four features that are subject to criticism.

1. Reliance on moral rhetoric to support one position and denounce the other

In the past, such rhetoric was conspicuous in church criticism of homosexuality, which was described as inevitably associated with all kinds of evil habits and lusts, from which, by implication, heterosexuality was protected. This indiscriminate condemnation contributed to the marginalisation and persecution of homosexuals. Decriminalisation and pastoral acceptance have not yet entirely eliminated this rhetoric from the language of church members. On the other hand many church reports now lean in the reverse direction and one detects efforts to compensate for the past sins of the churches.

The main examples now occur not among the critics but among the supporters of homosexuality. Here the case presented often consists largely of a range of 'good words', mostly moral qualities, associated with the one position and a range of 'bad words' with the other.

A recent example is that of a Presbyterian minister's preaching in his church on the subject of human sexuality. On the one hand he associated homosexuality with liberation, justice, openness, acceptance, freedom, love (indeed 'new heights of loving'), gentleness and truth. Those who disagreed were described as 'hounds of heaven', contravening human rights, obsessed with sex, ignorant and prejudiced, persecutors, with 'chains of oppression'. The sermon concluded with Lowell's moving hymn, 'Once to every man and nation' with its dramatic contrasts between 'strife of truth with falsehood, for the good or evil side'. The good side was then described in terms of 'bloom', 'light', and the 'brave'; the evil side was associated with 'blight', 'darkness', 'cowardice' and 'wrong'. The sermon left no doubt as to where all these terms applied. This may be regarded as powerful rhetoric, but it is certainly not argument.[1]

Often statements of this kind are, as in this case, followed by an appeal for people to sit down together and listen to one another. It is not surprising if this does not happen when one side monopolises the language of the moral high ground rather than presenting arguments with substantial moral or theological content. The well-known name for this procedure is 'argumentum ad hominem'—attack the opponent, not the argument.

It is important to abstain from any form of moral intimidation. Neither party in the debate has any moral monopoly, neither

today nor in their histories, and this procedure must be exposed for what it is and
replaced by real discussion with solid content.

2. There is no close correlation between morality and religion

The above rhetorical method assumes that
there is always an inbuilt relation between
moral rectitude and religious or theological
truth. In this sphere, if moral qualities we all
recognise (such as love, loyalty, unselfishness, etc.) are exhibited in the lives of homosexual partnerships, then it is argued that
this life-style must be acceptable to God, and
is indeed as much his gift and blessing as
heterosexual marriage. Right morality and
true religion, it is claimed, or more often just
implied, always go together.

Everyone's experience, in fact, contradicts
this assumption. We all know of admirable,
morally upright citizens of unblemished
character who are atheists or even strongly
anti-religious. And we know of the reverse—
the sincere and humble Christian who fights
an often losing battle against known moral
weaknesses or habits, be it alcoholism, klep-
tomania, a sexual fault, or bad temper, and
yet who knows the ever-renewed grace and

forgiveness of God in the way that is outside the atheist's ken.

Thus we may recognise that some homosexual partnerships exhibit more qualities of kindness, mutual support, etc., than some heterosexual marriages, and of course vice versa. Thus we can also recognise that a homosexual partnership may have helped someone to find acceptance, stability, responsibility, even deliverance from drugs, without this fact 'proving' that such a partnership is theologically acceptable as part of the divine pattern for creation.

I first learned this clearly when I had to accept the real rescue of a young man from hard drugs by the Unification Church or 'Moonies', in spite of the Christian theological criticism of its Asian syncretist beliefs. I accepted the moral achievement but rejected the associated theology. It would be so much simpler if moral quality always coincided with theological truth, but it doesn't, and any argument involving this assumption is simply invalid. The loving, permanent homosexual relationships of which we are told are irrelevant to the central theological issue.

3. We all have moral 'blind spots'

The presence of the above positive qualities among homosexuals is equally irrelevant to our moral judgment on this type of relationship itself. It is notorious that we are capable of great moral inconsistencies. The more dramatic examples occur when a devoted husband and father, pillar of the church and respected citizen noted for good works, is discovered to have embezzled clients' funds, secretly gambled or maintained a mistress, or otherwise acted 'out of character'. Defence lawyers often play on this very contrast, and the media make much of it. And in varying degrees there is some touch of Jekyll and Hyde in all of us. Which of us good 'law and order' people has never deliberately and knowingly broken the speed limit when the law is not looking?

A variation on this fact of inconsistency occurs when a person who is full of the virtues is felt to have a serious blind spot on certain moral issues. The animal rights supporter may approve of capital punishment; the ecological enthusiast may be an example of conspicuous consumer spending; the peace campaigner may adopt openly militant and violent methods. Each issue then has to be discussed on its own merits and it is no argument to point to one's virtues in other areas. So also with homosexual partnerships—they may be admirable in many other ways, but this has nothing to do with the inherent rightness or wrongness of such relationships.

4. Reliance on moral arguments in a pluralist culture

A weakness in the contemporary use of moral considerations to justify the homosexual case is that there is no agreed public moral reference point in modern Western culture. Objective moral standards of right and wrong have been eroded, and any theological or Christian base abandoned. Morality is said to derive from changing 'cultural values' and in a pluralist society where all moral standards are relative it reduces to a matter of personal, subjective opinion—my life-style and ethic alongside yours. Indeed this argument is invoked in support of a variety of sexual life-styles and behaviour, including homosexual relationships, as equally 'right' for different people.

The churches themselves are caught up in our own culture more than they know; their pronouncements in the field of sexuality often reflect the values of contemporary society rather than the gospel. This makes it all the more necessary—and difficult—to seek a base beyond the flux of contemporary culture in the classic theology of the Christian faith, and especially in what we believe about God and the pattern for human life that he has created. To this issue we now turn.

A THEOLOGICAL UNDERSTANDING OF GENDER

There are two possible views of God, each of which has a corresponding view of humanity and of gender. The Godhead is either

1. a unitary being and so non-relational within itself (i.e. monotheism); or
2. a more complex single being with differentiated (i.e. 'hetero') internal relations (as in trinitarianism).

The use of the terms 'homo' and 'hetero' is perhaps unusual in the theology of God and may seem contrived, but they do apply and serve to show the inter-relation between the theology of God, the theology of creation, especially of gender, and the ethics of our subject, especially of love. Let us now look at each position more closely, and try to spell this out.

1. Non-relational monotheism and a God of love

God has often been seen as a unitary being, with no internal structure to sustain inherent relationships. This view is called *monotheism*. There is nothing distinctively Christian in such a unitary view of God, for

Judaism, Islam and some other faiths would assent to it.

If such a God is to be eternally and inherently loving then this God has no eternal object to relate to in loving apart from himself. Such self-love we call narcissism and regard as unhealthy. To have an object to relate to in love, a unitarian God has to create human beings. This makes God dependent on us in order to be himself, instead of our depending on him in order to be fully ourselves. God is then less than an absolute, ultimate being who is love in himself; we humans enable him to love and to 'be' love. There is not much security for us in such a God, whose nature we determine.

Humanity, if made in the image of such a God, would also be essentially undifferentiated, unitary and all alike. (The technical terms for this are androgynous and hermaphrodite; nowadays we would say unisex.) Gender difference in this case would be reduced to the level of the biology needed for reproduction; it would have nothing to do with reflecting the nature of God. Therefore, if God is love, gender has no essential connection with the nature of love. Hence there is no real difference in hetero-relationships of love and homo-relationships of love.

Not surprisingly, therefore, supporters of

the homosexual position are often monotheistic in their theology, i.e. unitarians rather than trinitarians. This first came home to me when I read a paper on Christology (who and what Jesus is), written by a leading homosexual minister. He presented Jesus not as essentially divine but only as a outstanding prophet and teacher, whose death had no unique significance.[2] Jesus must then have worshipped a unitary 'God of love'; and there is no room in this view for the trinitarian view of God's nature. This unitarian view would not be accepted by churches associated with the World Council of Churches, by Christians of the Lausanne movement, or by the Catholic or Eastern Orthodox churches, but it comports well with the homosexual position.

It is this unitarian or monotheistic God who is usually invoked in statements that support homosexuality by declaring that God loves us all just as we are, no matter what our sexual orientation. We must expose this apparently unchallengeable declaration as most misleading. In the context of the sexuality discussion it always implies that God accepts, even loves, homosexuality itself, which is then declared to be another blessing from God.

I sincerely hope God does not love, and

so approve, any of us as we are in this undiscriminating fashion. There are things about myself that I regret, even hate. The Christian gospel is that God loves me *in spite of what I still am* in so many ways, that he is ready to forgive all this, and knows what he will yet make me through Christ with whom my future is hidden. That is the 'amazing grace' of God, the forgiveness that is misrepresented or entirely omitted in the common claim for the way God loves homosexuals and their homosexual activity. This sort of claim would support not only homosexual behaviour but every kind of human wrongdoing. It must be exposed for the distorting and dangerous half-truth that it is.

2. Hetero-relational trinitarian God: eternal love in its fullness

In turning to the heterosexual view we shall find that we are operating not in the moral categories of the homosexual supporters but in basic structural and relational categories both for God and for mankind i.e. in terms of how we are actually made.

The classic Christian position sets forth an internal self-differentiation within the Godhead, with God as Father, Son and Holy Spirit. This distinctive Christian doctrine of the Trinity is no mere speculative or archaic option to be discarded if we are to relate to modern culture. The present century has seen a massive re-discovery of the centrality of this understanding of God and today many of our major theologians have been producing substantial studies of the Trinity, the crown of Christian reflection about the faith. We have discovered that in the Christian view of persons we are *constituted by* our relations with others, our belongingness. We are not self-contained atomistic 'marbles' as modern individualism would have it; our critique of this false view derives from recognising that we are made in the image of our maker, a trinitarian God who is essentially relational.

Likewise, and for the same reasons, we reject the current political and economic views that society arises from a voluntary social contract between free individuals acting in their own interests. We can critique what has gone so manifestly wrong in Western societies only on the basis of an organic understanding of society as *constituted by* a network of relationships. Leonardo Boff, a leading Catholic exponent in South America of what is known as liberation theology, has a whole volume on *Trinity and society*. In it an impressive exposition of the classic doctrine of God is the basis for his radical critique of the oppression and poverty around him, and of both capitalism and socialism.

It is also of great significance that due to twentieth century developments in the science of physics, physicists no longer see the material world as made up of basic building blocks called atoms but rather in terms of interacting complexes. This is another sign that the hetero-relational or trinitarian view of God can provide the most comprehensive reference point and model for all thinking about the creation—the physical world, human society, and the human person.

In the trinitarian view God is not a three-in-one partnership of equal divine individuals, but one single divinity with internal self-differentiation into three 'persons' —differences for which we lack adequate human language but which we describe as Father, Son and Holy Spirit. These differences provide opportunity for a new form of love. This is not only reciprocal love between parties who are like each other; it goes further by reaching across the real and basic differences between the parties. This love is richer and deeper because it has the added dimension of complementarity. The parties now depend upon each other for their own completeness; each is actually *constituted by* relation in love with the two other different yet equal partners in the Godhead. They do not first exist and then have the option of loving; and they do not love their own mirror-images. What we have called 'hetero-relationship' goes beyond 'homo-relationship' into a mutual interweaving in love of the very being of each different 'party' with the basic reality of the two other 'parties'.

Co-humanity in the image of the Trinity

There are immediate and profound implications for our understanding of how this trinitarian God has created the human race. We now have the model for an internal differentiation basic to created humanity, seen in gender as male and female, and maintained in heterosexual but not in homosexual relations.

This is set forth in the first creation story in Genesis 1:26-27 where we read, 'God said, "Let us make humankind in our image, according to our likeness" . . . So . . . in the image of God he created them; male and female he created them.' This is repeated in Genesis 5:1-2. Here our likeness to God is not spelled out in terms of sharing in his spirituality, rationality, creativity, moral nature or righteousness, self-consciousness, power, free-will, knowledge or any other distinctive features that separate us from the animals. It is the fact of complementarity through gender that affirms the likeness.

This likeness, moreover, is not a point-to-point correspondence so that we start looking for a male and a female member within the Trinity and then proceed to impose gender or sexuality on God. It is, rather, an analogy where the complementary relationship between the genders is likened to the complementary relationships within the Trinity. Both God and human beings are essentially differentiated and relational in nature. This is the first and most important thing the story says about humans as the image of God; note that it is not simply identified with sexuality and reproduction, which are mentioned further on in the narrative. These are aspects of gender but not its essence, which is complementary relationship in wider dimensions than the sexual.

It is also important to note that whereas the animal world is created 'each according to their kind' or species, mankind is not divided into various species of race, cultures or societies, but simply into the two genders. These are not equivalent to two different species, since in their complementarity they need each other to form the one human species. It might be said that the homosexual position breaks this co-humanity up into two different species, 'hetero' and 'homo', each with its own 'sexual' orientation' and practices, although only the former is able to fulfill the associated Genesis duty to be fruitful and multiply.

The complementarity between man and woman is at the heart of the second more detailed creation story in Genesis 2:15-25, where again there is creation of community between man and woman, as equals but different. The key concept is in Genesis 2:18 where it is declared that it is unsatisfactory for man to be alone. His incompleteness is remedied not by the creation of another man like himself, but by the creation of a woman as a complementary being. Here again marriage and sexuality come later in the account, and are not to be confused with the gender that they presuppose.

In the light of the profound insights in these two creation accounts it might be said that the main task of the current feminist movement is to affirm the place of woman as the original, equal, distinctive, complementary and indispensable 'other' of man. The ultimate model for this is the Trinity.

Strangely, this relation of gender to exposition of the image of God eluded the great theological minds of the past. Augustine,

Aquinas and Calvin all tend to subsume gender under reproduction and marriage and to see the divine image in terms of our differences from the animals, as in the moral and intellectual categories we listed above. Only since the great German theologian Karl Barth took a major step forward in the middle of our century and related gender to the image of the Trinity have we been equipped to articulate a theology of gender, sexuality and marriage.

The complementarity of gender

It is of course true that there are many other kinds of complementarity between people especially where there is close friendship or love between man and man, or woman and woman. There are many forms of comlementary relationship—between manager and staff, oarsmen and cox, surgeon and anaesthetist, architect and builder, homekeeper and wage-earner, extrovert and introvert personalities, the practical and the thinker, the Marys and the Marthas. Any of these and many more may exist between the partners in a homosexual relationship, and may serve to support and enrich the quality of relationship. What then is so special about the complementarity of gender?

There are at least six dimensions in which gender stands apart from all other forms of complementarity, and we have already alluded to a number of these:

1. It is a given fact, unchangeable, and in no sense voluntary.

2. It is biologically necessary and every human being originates in gender, with a father and a mother. Here it serves that basic concern for survival at the heart of all societies; the sterile state of homosexuality ignores this concern and is in fact parasitical on a life-affirming society.

3. It is anatomically appropriate both for initial attraction through different kinds of beauty and for the fullest expressions of love-making. In comparison the options open to homosexuals are inadequate, often contrived, and in some of the commonest forms actually dangerous (will any medical school support anal intercourse?).

4. It touches every aspect of the psyche. In the words of the nineteenth century philosopher Feuerbach, it is 'a distinction which pervades the entire organism, which is everywhere present, which is infinite, and whose beginning and end are beyond discovery.' Somewhere here lies the mystique, the wonder, of what exists between a man and a woman in all relationships, in all degrees, whether married

or celibate, from the brief polite encounter at a ticket office to the ecstasies of love-making.

5. It is presented at the heart of both biblical creation accounts as we have examined them, and it runs through the Bible as a norm in counterpoint with the story of the destruction of complementarity through the effects of sin, and of its restoration through Christ.

6. It is theologically at the heart of the Christian doctrine of humanity as made in the image of the distinctively trinitarian God. Any theology of homosexuality will have to come to terms with this position. It would, however, seem impossible to present a homosexual partnership as an 'equally valid' alternative image of the Christian God without basic distortion of the rich trinitarian view into the inadequate monotheism of a 'God of love.'

Any one of these six features would be sufficient to establish the uniqueness of gender complementarity; taken together they present an overwhelming case for the special status of gender and of heterosexuality. Here there is an interlocking or bonding abundantly provided for in male and female as created that is absent from relations between two men or two women. No emphasis upon moral features or quality of relationship can replace this essential feature of complementary difference, lacking in the homosexual position.

The homosexual position, on the contrary, either ignores all that we have said about gender or regards it as of no importance and therefore separates it from sexuality and from both heterosexual marriage and homosexual partnership. But in practice gender often reasserts itself; in a gay or lesbian relationship it sometimes happens that one partner begins to assume the role or the appearance and behaviour conventionally associated with the opposite gender. And of course the unconscious ramifications of gender in the life of the homosexual person since birth cannot be escaped.

We now ask those who support the normalisation of homosexuality to avoid dependence on rhetoric or irrelevant moral considerations and to engage with the trinitarian understanding of God that defines the distinctively Christian position. Only in this way can there be a meeting of Christian minds in the current discussions.

NOTES

1. From the copy of a sermon given in Auckland, New Zealand, in November 1991 by

the Rev. David Clark, a prominent supporter of the comprehensive acceptance of homosexuality as a normal Christian position.

2. A paper on 'Who Jesus is for us today', submitted in New Zealand in 1991 by Dr David Bromell to a Methodist Church committee on doctrine. Through the media Dr Bromell has become nationally known as a homosexual minister. He is a former Baptist pastor seeking admission to the Methodist ministry.

RECOMMENDED READNG

D S Bailey, *The man-woman relationship in Christian thought* (Longmans, 1959). An older but comprehensive study.

The House of Bishops of the Church of England, *Issues in human sexuality*: a statement by the House of Bishops of the General Synod of the Church of England. (London: Church House, 1991). The most recent, and perhaps the best, of the church reports.

P K Jewett, *Man as male and female* (Grand Rapids: Eerdmans, 1975). A solid theological study.

Janet Martin Soskice (ed.), *After Eve* (Marshall/Pickering, 1990). See especially the essay by Paul Fiddes on Barth's position.

Samuel Terrien, *Till the heart sings: a biblical theology of manhood and womanhood* (Philadelphia: Fortress Press, 1985). A leading Old Testament scholar's charming account of gender and sexuality.

◆ Sane sex ◆

FRANCIS FOULKES

The argument of this book has been that our sexuality is a gift of God for the enrichment of our lives, individually and in our relationships. Medical science, psychology, and above all, human experience, combine to show the wisdom of the directions our Maker has given to us relating to our sexuality. We neglect them to our own great loss, and potentially do an incalculable disservice to the generation to come. We should be very cautious about coming to the conclusion that the teaching of the Scriptures, which from age to age has guided people in their living and life-style, is now outmoded merely because it comes from a time and culture remote from our own. The Roman Catholic biblical scholar, J P Meier, commenting on a contemporary report on human sexuality, says how too readily New Testament teaching is written off as 'time conditioned' when it indeed 'deserves more detailed and serious treatment'. He expresses a justifiable uneasiness with the

> tendency to dismiss as time bound any rigorous demand that offends the spirit of the moment. At times it may be we ourselves, rather than the New Testament, who deserve the warning label of time bound.[1]

Several of the writers who have contributed to in this book have emphasised that there is no place for judgmentalism in a genuinely Christian attitude. We all stand under the judgment—and the grace—of God. God's word, as it comes to us in the Scriptures, relating to many aspects of our lives, judges us. Nevertheless, it also brings the unchanging message of the outreaching love of God and the forgiveness offered to all who turn back to him. We see many in our society who, though responsible for their actions, are 'more sinned against than sinning', because of broken relationships and distorted values that they have inherited, and the pressures in society to conform to a way of life very far removed from 'sane sex'. The grace of God, however, means that new beginnings are possible. Life can be disentangled from those distorted values and there can be healing and renewal in the area of relationships. Inner strength to live the kind of life God intended is available from the Spirit of God.

It is supremely important that those who seek to follow the Christian sexual ethic should not despair of the disorder they find in the world. The often quoted Chinese proverb is apt, 'Don't curse the darkness, light a candle'. Much—and it is more than we can imagine—can be done by one person, one couple, one family. When Christian people, in the expression of their sexuality as in other ways, are salt and light in the world, they can achieve far more than committees or commissions, resolutions or regulations. We have the privilege and responsibility of seeking to live by God's wise and loving directions and of commending them to others. The Church has a vital teaching role to fulfil in these matters, and above all the task of offering an example to the world.

In essence the Christian sexual ethic is spelt out in terms of relationship and union. Whether for single or married people, the

most intimate relationship of all is found in
union with God. It means partnership based
on commitment and genuine love; a partnership of male and female, equal and complementary—in marriage, in society, and in the
life of the Church—for their own enrichment
and the enrichment of the world.

NOTE

1. J P Meier, *The vision of Matthew* (Paulist
Press, 1979), p.2.